First World War

and Army of Occupation

War Diary

France, Belgium and Germany

17 DIVISION
Headquarters, Branches and Services
Royal Army Veterinary Corps
Assistant Director Veterinary Services
15 July 1915 - 31 March 1919

WO95/1990/3

The Naval & Military Press Ltd
www.nmarchive.com
Published in association with The National Archives

Published by

The Naval & Military Press Ltd

Unit 10 Ridgewood Industrial Park,

Uckfield, East Sussex,

TN22 5QE England

Tel: +44 (0) 1825 749494

www.naval-military-press.com

www.nmarchive.com

This diary has been reprinted in facsimile from the original. Any imperfections are inevitably reproduced and the quality may fall short of modern type and cartographic standards.

Contents

Document type	Place/Title	Date From	Date To
Heading	WO95/1990/3		
Heading	17th Division A.D.V.S. Jly 1915-Mar 1919		
Heading	17th Division Headquarters 17th Division. A.D.V.S. Vol. I From 15th To 31st July 1915		
War Diary	Winchester	15/07/1915	15/07/1915
War Diary	Southampton	15/07/1915	15/07/1915
War Diary	Le Havre	16/07/1915	17/07/1915
War Diary	Lumbres	18/07/1915	18/07/1915
War Diary	Renescure	19/07/1915	19/07/1915
War Diary	Steenvoorde	20/07/1915	24/07/1915
War Diary	Reninghelst	25/07/1915	31/07/1915
Heading	17th Division Hd. Qrs. 17th Div. (A.D.V.S.) Vol: II August 15		
War Diary	Reninghelst	01/08/1915	31/08/1915
Heading	H.Q. 17th Div: A.D.V.S. Vol 3 Sept 15		
War Diary	Reninghelst	01/09/1915	30/09/1915
Heading	17th Division H.Q. 17th Div. A.D.V.S. Vol 4 Oct 15		
War Diary	Reninghelst	01/10/1915	06/10/1915
War Diary	Steenvoorde	07/10/1915	22/10/1915
War Diary	Reninghelst	23/10/1915	31/10/1915
Heading	17th Div H.Q. 17th Div. A.D.V.S. Vol. 5 Nov 15		
War Diary	Reninghelst	01/11/1915	30/11/1915
Heading	A.D.V.S. 17th Div. Vol 6 121/7928		
War Diary	Reninghelst	01/12/1915	31/12/1915
Heading	A.D.V.S. 17th Div. Vol: 7 Jan 1916		
War Diary	Reninghelst	01/01/1916	08/01/1916
War Diary	Tilques	09/01/1916	31/01/1916
Heading	A.D.V.S. 17th Division Vol VIII		
War Diary	Tilques	01/02/1916	05/02/1916
War Diary	Tatinghem	06/02/1916	07/02/1916
War Diary	Reninghelst	08/02/1916	29/02/1916
War Diary	17th Div ADVS Vol 9		
War Diary	Reninghelst	01/03/1916	07/03/1916
War Diary	Steenvoorde	08/03/1916	11/03/1916
War Diary	Merris	12/03/1916	23/03/1916
War Diary	Armentieres	24/03/1916	16/05/1916
War Diary	Tilques	17/05/1916	12/06/1916
War Diary	Allonville	13/06/1916	28/06/1916
War Diary	Mericourt	29/06/1916	04/07/1916
War Diary	Ville	05/07/1916	11/07/1916
War Diary	Cavillon	12/07/1916	15/07/1916
War Diary	Pont Remy	16/07/1916	23/07/1916
War Diary	Ribemont	24/07/1916	02/08/1916
War Diary	Albert	03/08/1916	13/08/1916
War Diary	Nr Buire	14/08/1916	15/08/1916
War Diary	Bernaville	16/08/1916	16/08/1916
War Diary	Doullens	17/08/1916	21/08/1916
War Diary	Henu	22/08/1916	31/08/1916
Heading	War Diary Sept 1916 of A.D.V.S. 17th Division. Vol 15		

War Diary	Henu	01/09/1916	22/09/1916
War Diary	St. Riquier	23/09/1916	30/09/1916
Heading	War Diary of A.D.V.S. 17 Division For October 1916 Vol 16		
War Diary	St Riquier	01/10/1916	06/10/1916
War Diary	Pas.	07/10/1916	22/10/1916
War Diary	Treux	23/10/1916	27/10/1916
War Diary	Citadel	28/10/1916	31/10/1916
Heading	War Diary A.D.V.S. 17 Divn & 29th M of Vas Section for November 1916 Vol 17		
War Diary	Minden Post	01/11/1916	14/11/1916
War Diary	Treux	15/11/1916	15/11/1916
War Diary	Cavillon	16/11/1916	30/11/1916
War Diary	In The Field		
War Diary	Cavillon	01/12/1916	13/12/1916
War Diary	Corbie	14/12/1916	25/12/1916
War Diary	In The Field	26/12/1916	31/12/1916
War Diary	A2d 9.7 Albert (Combined Sheet)	01/01/1917	15/01/1917
War Diary	In The Field	16/01/1917	16/01/1917
War Diary	Corbie	17/01/1917	26/01/1917
War Diary	In The Field	28/01/1917	31/01/1917
Heading	War Diary. of A.D.V.S (Major W.W.R. Neale A.V.C.) 17th Divn and. 29th Mobile Veterinary Sect. A.V.C. attd 17th Division for February 1917 Vol 20		
War Diary	In The Field F 18 C 3.3 Albert (Combined Sheet)	01/02/1917	20/02/1917
War Diary	In The Field	21/02/1917	28/02/1917
War Diary	Heilly	01/03/1917	02/03/1917
War Diary	Contay	03/03/1917	16/03/1917
War Diary	Willeman	17/03/1917	31/03/1917
War Diary	In The Field	01/04/1917	31/07/1917
War Diary	St. Nicholas	01/08/1917	31/08/1917
War Diary	In The Field	01/09/1917	31/12/1917
War Diary	In The Field Ytres	01/01/1918	01/01/1918
War Diary	In The Field Ytres & Bertincourt	01/02/1918	21/03/1918
War Diary	In The Field	22/03/1918	31/07/1918
War Diary	In The Field (Toutencourt)	01/08/1918	07/08/1918
War Diary	Allonville & Hamelet	08/08/1918	17/08/1918
War Diary	In The Field Toutencourt	18/08/1918	20/08/1918
War Diary	Lechelle	01/10/1918	06/10/1918
War Diary	Heudecourt	07/10/1918	09/10/1918
War Diary	Guillemin Farm	10/10/1918	10/10/1918
War Diary	Montigny	11/10/1918	16/10/1918
War Diary	In The Field	25/09/1918	30/09/1918
War Diary	Inchy	02/11/1918	05/11/1918
War Diary	Inchy Poix du Nord.	05/11/1918	05/11/1918
War Diary	Poix du Nord	05/11/1918	07/11/1918
War Diary	Poix du Nord-Locquignol	07/11/1918	07/11/1918
War Diary	Locquignol	07/11/1918	08/11/1918
War Diary	Aulnoye	08/11/1918	12/11/1918
War Diary	Aulnoye Vendecies	12/11/1918	12/11/1918
War Diary	Vendegies Inchy	13/11/1918	13/11/1918
War Diary	Inchy	13/11/1918	08/12/1918
War Diary	St. Gratien	09/12/1918	12/12/1918
War Diary	Hallencourt	13/12/1918	31/01/1919
War Diary	Cocqueril	01/02/1919	09/02/1919
War Diary	Hallencourt	09/02/1919	31/03/1919

WO 1990/8

17TH DIVISION

A. D. V. S.

JLY 1915-MAR 1919

17th Division

Headquarters 17th Division.

A. D. V. S.

Vol: I.

From 15th to 31st July 1915

Instructions regarding War Diaries and Intelligence Summaries are contained in F. S. Regs., Part II. and the Staff Manual respectively. Title Pages will be prepared in manuscript.

WAR DIARY
or
~~INTELLIGENCE SUMMARY~~

(Erase heading not required.)

Army Form C. 2118

of Major W. R. Neale A.V.C.
A.D.V.S. 17th Division

Place	Date	Hour	Summary of Events and Information	Remarks and references to Appendices
WINCHESTER	15/7/15	11.30 am	Left for SOUTHAMPTON	
SOUTHAMPTON	15/7/15	3 pm	Embarked on S.S. HUANCHACO	
LE HAVRE	16/7/15	2 am	Arrived and anchored for the night	
"	"	11.15 am	Commenced disembarking and finished by 2.30 pm	
"	17/7/15	7.00 am	Left HAVRE and proceeded by motor car to join Headquarters of 17th Division	
LUMBRES	18/7/15	8.30 am	Visited V.O. i/c G.H.Q and arranged with him for the collection of any sick animals left in his area - Proceeded to RENESCURE where billetted for the night - Visited by D.D.V.S. 2nd Army and given instructions.	
RENESCURE	19/7/15	9 am	Visited 51st Field Ambulance, 80th Brigade R.F.A and 81st Brigade R.F.A making arrangements at each place for leaving behind animals unable to proceed - Proceeded to HAZEBROUCK to report to D.D.V.S. and then on to STEENVOORDE - Visiting units at GODWAERSVELDE and CAESTRE. Billetted at STEENVOORDE	
STEENVOORDE	20/7/15		Visited by D.D.V.S. who inspected the Mobile Veterinary Section. Proceeded with DDVS to RENINGHELST to select a farm for the Mobile Veterinary section in the [illegible] Divisional area.	

1875 Wt. W593/826 1,000,000 4/15 J.B.C. & A. A.D.S.S./Forms/C. 2118.

2

Instructions regarding War Diaries and Intelligence Summaries are contained in F. S. Regs., Part II. and the Staff Manual respectively. Title Pages will be prepared in manuscript.

WAR DIARY
or
INTELLIGENCE SUMMARY
(Erase heading not required.)

Of Major W. R. Meale A.V.C. A.D.V.S. 17th Division

Army Form C. 2118

Place	Date	Hour	Summary of Events and Information	Remarks and references to Appendices
STEENVOORDE	22+23 7/15		Visiting & inspecting horses and mules of various units in the Division	
"	24/7/15		Left STEENVOORDE for RENINGHELST. Headquarters of Division established at the latter place. Attended at No 46 Mob: Vet: Sectn to see a demonstration by Lieut. HOBDAY on the intra-dermal palpebral method of malleinisation	
RENINGHELST	25/7/15 to 28/7/15		Doing ordinary duty inspecting & visiting units. The Division not all up in its proper area and long distances had to be covered. From the time of disembarking up to the present a large number of neck galls occurred amongst both horses and mules under the Zinc pad over which the neck strap passes. Some of these were very serious and had to be evacuated to the Base. Kicks and rope galls also very prevalent.	
"	29/7/15		~~A.D.V.S. 2nd Army~~ General WINTER accompanied by D.D.V.S. 2nd Army inspected No 29 Mobile Veterinary Section.	
"	30 & 31 7/15		Routine inspection of units & Mob: Vet: Sect.	

W. R. Meale Major A.V.C.
A.D.V.S. 17th Division

17th Division

121/6874

Hd: Qrs: 17th Div: (A.D.V.S.)

Vol: II

August 15

Sheet No 1.

Instructions regarding War Diaries and Intelligence Summaries are contained in F. S. Regs., Part II. and the Staff Manual respectively. Title Pages will be prepared in manuscript.

WAR DIARY
or
~~INTELLIGENCE~~ SUMMARY
(Erase heading not required.)

of Major W R Meale A.V.C. Army Form C. 2118
A.D.V.S. 17th Division

Place	Date	Hour	Summary of Events and Information	Remarks and references to Appendices
RENINGHELST	1/8/15		Proceeded to ARQUES to investigate the case of a mule left with a MONSR DUBISSON. Found that it was left on July 11th by the 15th Division and was collected by V.O i/c G.H.Q on 25/7/15	
"	2/8/15		Proceeded to TERDEGHEM to inspect two horses of 17th Div: Cyclists. Both suffering from Rope gall. Ordered O.C. 29 M.V.S. to collect the worst case tomorrow.	
"	3/8/15		Inspecting animals of 78th Brigade R.F.A. and 78th Field Compy R.E. Proceeded to FLETRE to inspect two horses left behind by 80th Brigade R.F.A. Ordered O.C. 29 M.V.S to collect them tomorrow.	
"	4/8/15		Inspecting 50th 51st and 52nd Infantry Brigade animals.	
"	5/8/15		Visited 29 M.V.S. Inspecting animals of 17th Divl Train. D.D.V.S. 2nd Army interviewed the L/cpls attached to the three Infantry Brigades.	
"	6/8/15		Visited 17th Divisional Ammunition Column at HONDEGHEM. This unit moving to BOESCHEPE. Made arrangements for 3 mules and 1 horse unfit to travel to be left with MONSR HENRI MASSIET.	
"	7/8/15		Received letter Q.M.G. G.H.Q. Q/2061 cancelling issue of Motor Car for A.D.V.S. Visited Mobile Veterinary Section. Office work.	
"	8/8/15		Inspecting animals of 80th Brigade R.F.A	

1875 Wt. W593/826 1,000,000 4/15 J.B.C. & A. A.D.S.S./Forms/C. 2118.

Sheet No 2.

Instructions regarding War Diaries and Intelligence Summaries are contained in F. S. Regs., Part II. and the Staff Manual respectively. Title Pages will be prepared in manuscript.

WAR DIARY

~~or~~

~~INTELLIGENCE SUMMARY~~

(Erase heading not required.)

of Major W. R. Meale A.V.C. A.D.V.S. 17th Division

Army Form C. 2118

Place	Date	Hour	Summary of Events and Information	Remarks and references to Appendices
RENINGHELST	9/8/15		Inspecting 51st Field Ambulance, 17th Signal Compy R.E., 77th 78th and 93rd Field Comps R.E.	
"	10/8/15		Inspecting Headquarter horses. D.D.V.S. called in afternoon and asked if I could recommend Capt. R. TINDLE A.V.C. for position of A.D.V.S. of a Division. Visited 37th Division M.V.S. to enquire if they had collected the 3 mules and 1 horse left at HONDEGHEM. Informed that the three mules had been collected but the horse was still left on the farm as it was unable to be moved.	
"	11/8/15		Inspecting animals of 78th Brigade R.F.A.	
"	12/8/15		Issuing Remounts with D.A.Q.M.G. Visited M.V.S.	
"	13/8/15		Office work and held Conference of the V.O's of the Division	
"	14/8/15		Inspecting York & Lancs (Pioneer Batt^n) animals also 17th Div^l Amm^n Col:	
"	15/8/15		Inspecting animals on farms at BOESCHEPE occupied by 17th Div^l Train. Found the animals on two of the farms to be suffering from Foot and Mouth Disease (Aphthous Fever)	
"	16/8/15		Superintending the disinfection of Horses feet and wagon wheels as they vacating the farms affected with Foot & Mouth Disease. Visited Mobile Vet: Sect. D.D.V.S. called re the outbreak of Foot & Mouth Disease & left "Out of Bounds" Cards &c.	

Sheet No 3.

Instructions regarding War Diaries and Intelligence Summaries are contained in F. S. Regs., Part II. and the Staff Manual respectively. Title Pages will be prepared in manuscript.

WAR DIARY

~~or~~

~~INTELLIGENCE SUMMARY~~

(Erase heading not required.)

of Major W.R. Neale A.V.C.
A.D.V.S. 17th Division

Army Form C. 2118

Place	Date	Hour	Summary of Events and Information	Remarks and references to Appendices
RENINGHELST	17/8/15		Interviewed MAIRE of BOESCHEPE re outbreak of Foot & Mouth Disease. Getting roads closed and farms placarded with "Out of Bounds" cards. Visited Mob: Vet: Sect.	
"	18/8/15		Inspecting animals of 81st Brigade R.F.A. Foot and Mouth Disease reported at the BRASSERIE – BOESCHEPE. ~~Visited~~ Inspected the animals and found them to be diseased.	
"	19/8/15		Inspecting 79th Brigade R.F.A.	
"	20/8/15		Conference with V.O's of the Division. Visited by D.D.V.S. and went to 78th Brigade R.F.A. Am: Col: and No 1 Company 17th Div: Train with him and investigated the possibility of farriers making up shoes from old ones if they had field forges and anvils	
"	21/8/15		Inspecting animals of 51st Infantry Brigade. Issuing Remounts with D.A.A.M.S.	
"	22/8/15		Inspecting 52nd and 53rd Field Ambulance. Office work.	
"	23/8/15		Visited Mob: Vet: Sect:– Inspecting animals of 17th Divisional Train.	
"	24/8/15		Routine work. Received copy of telegram D.V. 30 d/23/8/15 directing that Capt R. TINDLE A.V.C. Commanding 29 Mobile Veterinary Section proceed to 6th Division on appointment as A.D.V.S. Lieut J.J. KEPPLE A.V.C. being sent to take over command of 29 Mob: Vet: Sect.	

1875 Wt. W593/826 1,000,000 4/15 J.B.C. & A. A.D.S.S./Forms/C. 2118.

Sheet No 4

WAR DIARY

~~WAR DIARY~~ ~~or~~ ~~INTELLIGENCE SUMMARY~~

(*Erase heading not required.*)

of Major W R Meale AVC ADVS 17th Division

Army Form C. 2118

Instructions regarding War Diaries and Intelligence Summaries are contained in F. S. Regs., Part II. and the Staff Manual respectively. Title Pages will be prepared in manuscript.

Place	Date	Hour	Summary of Events and Information	Remarks and references to Appendices
RENINGHELST	25/8/15		Inspecting animals of 79th Brigade R.F.A	
"	26/8/15		Inspecting Headquarter horses. Visited Mob: Vet: Sect. Proceeded to YPRES to attend to a horse of 52nd Field Ambulance wounded by a shell.	
"	27/8/15		Capt. R. TINDLE. A.V.C left the 29 Mob: Vet: Sect. on appointment as A.D.V.S 6th Division. Inspecting animals of 78th Brigade R.F.A. Lieut J.J. KEPPEL. A.V.C arrived and took over command of No 29 M.V.S vice Capt R. TINDLE AVC.	
"	28/8/15		Visited Mob: Vet: Sect. Office work.	
"	29/8/15		Visited Mob: Vet: Sect. Office work	
"	30/8/15		Inspecting animals of 80th Brigade R.F.A.	
"	31/8/15		Inspecting animals of 17th Divisional Ammunition Column	

W R Meale Major AVC
ADVS 17th Division

1875 Wt. W593/826 1,000,000 4/15 J.B.C. & A. A.D.S.S./Forms/C. 2118.

121/7592

K

H.Q. 17th Div: A.D.V.S.

Vol 3

Sept 15

Instructions regarding War Diaries and Intelligence Summaries are contained in F. S. Regs., Part II. and the Staff Manual respectively. Title Pages will be prepared in manuscript.

1st Sheet

WAR DIARY
or
~~INTELLIGENCE SUMMARY~~
(Erase heading not required.)

of Major W. R. Neale A.V.C
A.D.V.S. 17th Division

Army Form C. 2118

Place	Date	Hour	Summary of Events and Information	Remarks and references to Appendices
RENINGHELST	1.9.15		Inspection duty - Investigating the matter of Regimental Cookers and the dropping of nails on roads and elsewhere -	
"	2.9.15		Inspection duty and visiting farms in connection with Foot and Mouth disease.	
"	3.9.15		Routine work - Visited 29 Mob. Vet: Sect. and visited a new farm it is proposed to move the section into -	
"	4.9.15		Visiting different units of the Division and going into the question of horse standings for the winter - The 50th Inf: Bde transport lines in a low lying wet field and advised a change of camp.	
"	5th 6 & 8th 9.15	~~7~~	Routine work -	
"	9.9.15		Several A.V.C. Sergeants joined the Division for duty under the new scheme of having one Sergeant of the A.V.C. with each Inf. Bde and one for each Battery of Artillery and Brigade Ammunition Column & one for each Section of the Divisional Amn Col:	
"	10.9.15		More A.V.C Sergeants arrived for duty - Investigating cause of recent cases of Laminitis in 50th Inf: Bde - Found that some sacks of oats contained a large proportion of wheat - Advised that the whole of the oats be mixed together so as to make the proportion of wheat with each feed very small -	

1875 Wt. W593/826 1,000,000 4/15 J.B.C. & A. A.D.S.S./Forms/C. 2118.

2nd Sheet.

Instructions regarding War Diaries and Intelligence Summaries are contained in F. S. Regs., Part II. and the Staff Manual respectively. Title Pages will be prepared in manuscript.

WAR DIARY ~~or INTELLIGENCE SUMMARY~~ of Major W. R. Neal A.V.C. A.D.V.S. 17th Division

(Erase heading not required.)

Army Form C. 2118

Place	Date	Hour	Summary of Events and Information	Remarks and references to Appendices
RENINGHELST	11.9.15		Collecting a horse from the farm of Mons DESIRE HOUVENAGHEL at BOESCHEPE which was claimed by a Madam DELANDRE to have been given to her by Major E.D. MILLER Northamptonshire Yeomanry with whom it was left by a Canadian Officer. Conference in evening of administrative staff from 9 to 11.15 pm. Brought up question of the Wheat amongst the oats also that horses getting short hay ration owing to the trusses not weighing what they are issued at.	
"	12.9.15		Camp occupied by a part of No 3 Section 17th D.A.C. found to have Cattle on it affected with Foot + Mouth Disease. Gave orders for removal from the farm and usual disinfection.	
"	13.9.15		Routine work. Found that Lieut: W.J.C. KENNEY. A.V.C. had reported sick the night before and that he had been sent to HAZEBROUCK suffering from Diarrhoea. Probable duration of sickness one week.	
"	14.9.15		Routine work.	
"	15.9.15		With D.A.Q.M.G. to meet D.D.R. who inspected No 1 and 2 Camps 17th Div: Train, No 3 Comp: 17th D.A.C. and "A" Squadron Yorkshire Dragoons. Then to the Field Remount Section and selected horses for different units of the Division.	
"	16.9.15		Routine work. Visited by D.D.V.S. No 29 Mob: Vet: Sect: moved into a new farm where there is more shelter for the horses for the winter.	
"	17.9.15		Routine work. Conference of all V.O's of the Division	

1875 Wt. W593/826 1,000,000 4/15 J.B.C. & A. A.D.S.S./Forms/C. 2118.

3rd Sheet.

Instructions regarding War Diaries and Intelligence Summaries are contained in F. S. Regs., Part II. and the Staff Manual respectively. Title Pages will be prepared in manuscript.

WAR DIARY of Major W. R. Neale A.V.C. A.D.V.S. 17th Division

or

~~INTELLIGENCE SUMMARY~~

(*Erase heading not required.*)

Army Form C. 2118

Place	Date	Hour	Summary of Events and Information	Remarks and references to Appendices
RENINGHELST	18.9.15		Routine work.	
"	19.9.15		Routine work - Learned that Lieut W. G. C. KENNEY A.V.C. was evacuated sick to the Base - Informed D.D.V.S. of this by wire -	
"	20.9.15		Routine work.	
"	21.9.15		Routine work - Attended conference of the Administrative Staff of the Division - Applied for Veterinary Officer to replace Lieut: KENNEY	
"	22.9.15		Issuing Remounts with D.A.D.R.S. - Took O.C. 29 Mob: Vet: Sect: to the Sanitary Exhibition at BAILLEUL.	
"	23rd to 26th 9.15.		Routine work.	
"	27.9.15		D.D.V.S. came and met Lieut. A JACKSON A.V.C. by appointment - Lieut: JACKSON signed new agreement to continue his services -	
"	28.9.15		No. S.E 6655 Cpl H. YATES A.V.C. my clerk admitted to 52nd Field Ambulance with chronic Rheumatism - Received report from O.C. 17th D.A.C. re Lieut: F.K. HENTON A.V.C. and the way he spoke to O.C. No 3 Company 17th D.A.C.	
"	29.9.15		Visited Lieut: HENTON AVC and spoke to him about his conduct & the way to treat Senior Officers - Went on to HAZEBROUCK and reported the facts to D.D.V.S.	
"	30.9.15		Routine work. D.D.V.S. called and asked for a written report about Lieut: HENTON	

W.R.Neale Major AVC
A.D.V.S. 17th Div.

1875 Wt. W593/826 1,000,000 4/15 J.B.C. & A. A.D.S.S./Forms/C. 2118.

17th Division

K

121/7597

H.Q. 17th Div: A.D.V.S.

Vol 4

Oct 15

3rd
Em.

1st Sheet.

Instructions regarding War Diaries and Intelligence Summaries are contained in F. S. Regs., Part II. and the Staff Manual respectively. Title Pages will be prepared in manuscript.

WAR DIARY ~~or~~ ~~INTELLIGENCE SUMMARY~~ of Major W. R. Neale A.V.C. A.D.V.S. 17th Division

(Erase heading not required.)

Army Form C. 2118

Place	Date	Hour	Summary of Events and Information	Remarks and references to Appendices
RENINGHELST	1.10.15		Routine work - Found 2 Cows affected with Foot & Mouth Disease on the farm of Mme BODDAVET of BOESCHEPE occupied by "B" and "C" Battery wagon lines 78th Bde R.F.A. - Reported to D.D.V.S. 2nd Army and A.D.M.S. 17th Division.	
"	2.10.15		Routine work. D.D.V.S. called on Lieut. F.K. HENTON A.V.C.	
"	3.10.15		Issuing Remounts to units with D.A.A.M.G. - Lieut: P.S. SPARLING. AVC reported for duty in the place of Lieut: W.G.C. KENNEY invalided.	
"	4.10.15		Routine work.	
"	5.10.15		Routine work - A.D.V.S. 24th Division called as they are going to take over the billets occupied by the 17th Division - Part of the Division moving.	
"	6.10.15		The Division moving - Left RENINGHELST and arrived STEENVOORDE. Gave A.D.V.S. 24th Divn information of 2 horses left behind and also informed D.D.V.S. Received letter VF99 d/ 5/10/15 stating that Lieut: W.G.C. KENNEY AVC was invalided to England on 26.9.15.	
STEENVOORDE	7.10.15		Went to HAZEBROUCK with D.A.A.M.G. to ask D.D.R. for remounts. Called on D.D.V.S. Selecting Remounts at the Field Remount Section.	
"	8.10.15		Routine work.	
"	9.10.15		Inspection of all units of the 81st Brigade R.F.A. by D.D.V.S. 2nd Army who also inspected the 17th D.A.C. and visited the 29th Mobile Veterinary Section.	

2nd Sheet.

Instructions regarding War Diaries and Intelligence Summaries are contained in F. S. Regs., Part II. and the Staff Manual respectively. Title Pages will be prepared in manuscript.

WAR DIARY ~~or~~ ~~INTELLIGENCE SUMMARY~~

(*Erase heading not required.*)

of Major W. R. Neale A.V.C. ADVS. 17th Division

Army Form C. 2118

Place	Date	Hour	Summary of Events and Information	Remarks and references to Appendices
STEENVOORDE	10.10.15		Routine work - Selecting farm for the Mob: Vet: Sect.	
"	11.10.15		Routine work. Mobile Section moved into new farm so as to be more central. Inspected horse left at HERZEELE by 24th Division and gave orders to OC. 29 M.V.S. to collect it tomorrow.	
"	12th + 13th 10.15		Routine work.	
"	14.10.15		DDVS. called. With ADR. inspecting animals submitted to him for casting	
"	15th + 16th 10.15		Routine work.	
"	17.10.15		Visiting farms at ST. SYLVESTRE CAPPEL and EECKE occupied by units of our Division which DDVS. notified me were affected with Foot & Mouth disease.	
"	18.10.15		Routine work. Going into the question of getting the full hay allowance for horses as the Supplies only issue 10 lbs hay which is always short weight & the horses should get 12 lbs daily	
"	19.10.15		Routine work -	
"	20.10.15		Routine work. Received Secret Operation order re move of the Division - went to see position of Mob: Vet: Sect. in our new area.	
"	21.10.15		Routine work. ADVS. 3rd Division called to see position of Mob: Vet: Sect. for his Division which is relieving ours.	

1875 Wt. W593/826 1,000,000 4/15 J.B.C. & A. A.D.S.S./Forms/C. 2118.

Instructions regarding War Diaries and Intelligence Summaries are contained in F. S. Regs., Part II. and the Staff Manual respectively. Title Pages will be prepared in manuscript.

3rd Sheet.

WAR DIARY

or

~~INTELLIGENCE SUMMARY~~

(Erase heading not required.)

of Major W. R. Neale A.V.C. ADVS. 17th Division

Army Form C. 2118

Place	Date	Hour	Summary of Events and Information	Remarks and references to Appendices
STEENVOORDE	22.10.15		Moved to RENINGHELST	
RENINGHELST	23.10.15		Routine work.	
"	24.10.15		Routine work. Mobile Section moved up into its new position - Six men arrived from No 8 Vet: Hospl for duty with 29 M.V.S. in exchange for six men of the Section to be sent to No. 8 Vet: Hospl.	
"	25.10.15		Routine work.	
"	26.10.15		Routine work - Six men left 29 M.V.S. in exchange for the six who came from No 8 Vet: Hospl.	
"	27.10.15		H. M. The King inspected detachments of Vth Corps troops at RENINGHELST. Routine work.	
"	28.10.15		Routine work.	
"	29.10.15		Routine work. DDVS. Called and described a disease among horses of the 9th H. Bde Am: Col: supposed to be Cerebro Spinal Meningitis.	
"	30.10.15		Routine work - Visited horses of 9th H. Bde A.C. to see the symptoms of the disease	
"	31.10.15		Routine work.	

W R Neale Major AVC
ADVS. 17th Div.

1875 Wt. W593/826 1,000,000 4/15 J.B.C. & A. A.D.S.S./Forms/C. 2118.

HQ. 17th Div.
A.D.V.S.
Vol: 5

121
7634

11th Jan

K

Nov 15.

Instructions regarding War Diaries and Intelligence Summaries are contained in F. S. Regs., Part II. and the Staff Manual respectively. Title Pages will be prepared in manuscript.

Sheet 1

WAR DIARY ~~or INTELLIGENCE SUMMARY~~

(Erase heading not required.)

of Major W R [illegible] AVC
ADVS. 17th Division

Army Form C. 2118

Place	Date	Hour	Summary of Events and Information	Remarks and references to Appendices
RENINGHELST	1/11/15		Routine work. DDVS. Called re the re-engagement of Lieut: H.S. HOWARD JONES AVC. Very wet and roads & fields in a very soft muddy condition.	
"	2/11/15		Received notice from DAAMG that 29 Mob: Vet: Sect: is required to move from its present position as it is not at present in our Divisional Area and is required by the 9th Division. Later got instructions that it must move by noon tomorrow. Trying to find a new farm for the section but not successful as the area is very congested. Very wet and ground waterlogged.	
"	3/11/15		Moved 29 Mobile Section into a new farm. Routine work. Showery. Ground in very bad condition.	
"	4/11/15		Routine work. Fine but ground very soft & wet.	
"	5/11/15		Issuing Remounts with DAAMG. Conference with Veterinary Officers of the Division. Ground sodden and very muddy.	
"	6/11/15		Went to see two horses of 'C' Battery 79th Brigade which Lt Hill at the Conference yesterday evening said he would like me to inspect. Diagnosed one case as Acute Glanders and the other very suspicious. The DDVS 2nd Army was in the vicinity and he inspected the animals and concurred with my diagnosis. Destroyed and held Post Mortem examination of the acute case. There was ulceration of both nostrils but no macroscopic lesions in the lungs. Tested 51 horses of the Battery. 18 received the intra dermal palpebral injection as	

1875 Wt. W593/826 1,000,000 4/15 J.B.C. & A. A.D.S.S./Forms/C. 2118.

Sheet 2

Army Form C. 2118

WAR DIARY

~~or~~

~~INTELLIGENCE SUMMARY~~

(Erase heading not required.)

of Major W.W.R. Neale A.V.C.
A.D.V.S. 17th Division

Instructions regarding War Diaries and Intelligence Summaries are contained in F. S. Regs., Part II. and the Staff Manual respectively. Title Pages will be prepared in manuscript.

Place	Date	Hour	Summary of Events and Information	Remarks and references to Appendices
RENINGHELST	6/11/15		as well as the subcutaneous injection	
"	7/11/15		Visiting malleined horses of "C" Battery 79th Brigade R.F.A. D.D.V.S. 2nd Army called and saw the malleined horses.	
"	8/11/15		Visiting malleined horses of "C" Battery 79th Brigade R.F.A. Six reacted namely three to the subcutaneous neck injection and three to the intra-dermal palpebral injection. The latter three did not react to the subcutaneous neck injection but the eye reaction was very distinct. D.D.V.S. called and gave instructions for the destruction of the six reactors. Inspecting 180 mules which are being transferred from 17th Divisional Column to the Indian Corps. Malleined 45 more horses of "C" Battery 79th Brigade R.F.A.	
"	9/11/15		Inspecting malleined horses of "C" Battery 79th Brigade. Making post mortem examination on the six reactors. Glanders nodules found in both lungs of all six horses. Malleined 30 more horses completing the Battery. Informed the A.D.M.S. and Belgian Liaison Officer that Glanders exists on the farm G 22 b 8.7 map 28 occupied by "C" Battery 79th Brigade R.F.A. Received great assistance from Lieutenant T. T. G. KEPPEL A.V.C. during the testing and post mortem examinations.	

1875 Wt. W593/826 1,000,000 4/15 J.B.C. & A. A.D.S.S./Forms/C. 2118.

Sheet 3.

WAR DIARY ~~or~~ ~~INTELLIGENCE SUMMARY~~

(Erase heading not required.)

of Major W.W.R Neale A.V.C. A.D.V.S. 17th Division

Army Form C. 2118

Instructions regarding War Diaries and Intelligence Summaries are contained in F. S. Regs., Part II. and the Staff Manual respectively. Title Pages will be prepared in manuscript.

Place	Date	Hour	Summary of Events and Information	Remarks and references to Appendices
RENINGHELST.	10/11/15		Inspecting mallenied horses of "C" Battery 79th Brigade R.F.A twice during day. Visited D.A.D.O.S re nose bags, hay nets and head ropes for the Battery. DDVS called and inspected the mallenied horses. Disinfecting standings &c of "C" Battery 79th Brigade R.F.A. – Thunder, lightning, hail and ground in very muddy condition	
"	11/11/15		Inspecting mallenied horses of "C" Battery 79th Brigade R.F.A twice during the day. One doubtful reaction which was isolated for retesting. All the others passed the test. Inspected 58 mules of the 17th Divisional Ammunition Column which are being transferred to Indian Corps. DDVS called in the evening.	
"	12/11/15		Conference with all Veterinary Officers of the Division –	
"	13/11/15		Report on recent outbreak of Glanders to D.D.V.S. 2nd Army.	
"	14/11/15		Inspection duty. Sent a case of Mange (Psoroptic) from "A" Battery 80th Brigade R.F.A. to No 29 Mobile Veterinary Section	
"	15/11/15		Inspection duty. Collecting rings off old head ropes for D.D.V.S.	
"	16/11/15		Inspection duty. D.D.V.S. called. Captain F.K. HENTON A.V.C. went on leave home for 8 days.	

1875 Wt. W593/826 1,000,000 4/15 J.B.C. & A. A.D.S.S./Forms/C. 2118.

Sheet 4.

WAR DIARY

~~or~~

~~INTELLIGENCE SUMMARY~~

(Erase heading not required.)

of Major W.W.R. Neale A.V.C.
A.D.V.S. 17th Division

Army Form C. 2118

Instructions regarding War Diaries and Intelligence Summaries are contained in F. S. Regs., Part II. and the Staff Manual respectively. Title Pages will be prepared in manuscript.

Place	Date	Hour	Summary of Events and Information	Remarks and references to Appendices
RENINGHELST	17/11/15		Inspection duty. Classifying horses of 52nd Infantry Brigade for the purpose of the forage ration.	
"	18/11/15		Inspection duty	
"	19/11/15		With D.D.R. casting horses for Remount reasons. Inspection duty. Found one horse handed over to the 17th Divisional Ammunition Column by the Indian Corps in exchange for mules to be suffering from mange. Three of these horses came up with leather soles [illegible] and when the shoes were removed pus was discharging. Several were very thin and had to be sent to the [illegible] Section.	
"	20/11/15 21/11/15	}	Inspection duty.	
"	22/11/15		Malleined the original suspicious case and the doubtful reactor of "C" Battery 79th Brigade by the intra dermal palpebral method. D.D.V.S. called in the evening	
"	23/11/15		Inspecting the two malleined horses. The original suspect showing a good reaction the other not reacting. Getting the teams of Indian Corps horses amongst	

1875 Wt. W593/826 1,000,000 4/15 J.B.C. & A. A.D.S.S./Forms/C. 2118.

Sheet 5.

WAR DIARY
or
~~INTELLIGENCE~~ SUMMARY
(Erase heading not required.)

of Major W W R Meale AVC.
ADVS. 17th Division

Army Form C. 2118

Instructions regarding War Diaries and Intelligence Summaries are contained in F. S. Regs., Part II. and the Staff Manual respectively. Title Pages will be prepared in manuscript.

Place	Date	Hour	Summary of Events and Information	Remarks and references to Appendices
RENINGHELST	23/11/15		amongst which the mange case occurred clipped.	
"	24/11/15		Post Mortem Examination on horse of "C" Battery 79th Brigade R.F.A. which reacted to mallein. Glanders nodules in both lungs. Inspection duty.	
"	25/11/15		With D.A.Q.M.G. issuing Remounts to units. Inspection duty. LIEUTENANT W. R. HILL AVC reported that a horse of "C" Battery 79th Brigade R.F.A which died from Enteritis showed Glanders nodules in both lungs.	
"	26/11/15		Conference with Veterinary Officers of the Division.	
"	27/11/15 28/11/15 29/11/15 30/11/15		Inspection duty.	
			During the month the ground was very muddy and in a very bad state in fields where horses are picketed. Several cases of so called frost bite (Necrotic heels) occurred amongst the horses during the month.	
			W. W. R. Meale Major AVC. ADVS. 17th Division	

1875 Wt. W593/826 1,000,000 4/15 J.B.C. & A. A.D.S.S./Forms/C. 2118.

Sheet No 1.

Instructions regarding War Diaries and Intelligence Summaries are contained in F. S. Regs., Part II. and the Staff Manual respectively. Title Pages will be prepared in manuscript.

WAR DIARY

~~INTELLIGENCE SUMMARY~~

(Erase heading not required.)

of Major W. W. R. Neale A.V.C. ADVS. 17th Division

Army Form C. 2118

Place	Date	Hour	Summary of Events and Information	Remarks and references to Appendices
RENINGHELST	1/12/15		Routine work – Tested 28 horses of "C" Battery 79th Bde R.F.A. with mallein dilute by intra dermal palpebral method.	
"	2/12/15		Routine work – Inspected twice during the day the horses undergoing the mallein test. No reactions up to 24th hour –	
"	3/12/15		Inspecting malleined horses. No reactions in the first series – Conference with V.O's of the Division. D.D.V.S. called – 26 more horses (series 2) of "C" 79th Bde malleined –	
"	4/12/15		Visited malleined horses twice during the day – One horse of series 2 reacting – 40 more horses (series 3) of "C" 79 malleined –	
"	5/12/15		Visited malleined horses. Destroyed reactor in series 2 and made P.M. Ex nodules found in both lungs. D.D.V.S. came and saw the lungs. Malleined 32 more horses (series 4) completing the Battery.	
"	6/12/15		Visited malleined horses twice during the day. No reactions in series 3 and none of series 4 up to the 24th hour. Routine work	

1875 Wt. W593/826 1,000,000 4/15 J.B.C. & A. A.D.S.S./Forms/C. 2118.

Sheet No 2

Instructions regarding War Diaries and Intelligence Summaries are contained in F. S. Regs., Part II. and the Staff Manual respectively. Title Pages will be prepared in manuscript.

WAR DIARY
or
~~INTELLIGENCE SUMMARY~~
(Erase heading not required.)

Of Major W. W. R. Neale A.V.C. ADVS. 17th Division

Army Form C. 2118

Place	Date	Hour	Summary of Events and Information	Remarks and references to Appendices
RENINGHELST	7/12/15		Visited malleined horses. No reactions in cases 4 - Routine work.	
"	8/12/15		Routine work.	
"	9/12/15		Routine work.	
"	10/12/15		Issued experimental head ropes (rope reinforced with wire) to units to put on horses and mules which are known rope eaters. Conference with V.O's of the Division.	
"	11/12/15		Routine work. Went to HAZEBROUCK and told D.D.V.S. of projected move back of the D.A.C. with their horses and mules and some horses of the Divisional Artillery not wanted at the front at present.	
"	12/12/15		Issuing Remounts.	
"	13/12/15		Routine work.	
"	14/12/15		Conference with V.O's of the Division prior to my going on leave. Ordered exchange between Sergt RAY of the D.A.C. and Sergt LING attached A/79 with approval of the D.D.V.S.	

1875 Wt. W593/826 1,000,000 4/15 J.B.C. & A. A.D.S.S./Forms/C. 2118.

Sheet No 3

Instructions regarding War Diaries and Intelligence Summaries are contained in F. S. Regs., Part II. and the Staff Manual respectively. Title Pages will be prepared in manuscript.

WAR DIARY
or
~~INTELLIGENCE SUMMARY~~
(Erase heading not required.)

of Major [illegible] Neale AVC
ADVS 17th Division

Army Form C. 2118

Place	Date	Hour	Summary of Events and Information	Remarks and references to Appendices
~~[illegible]~~	15/12/15 to 23/12/15		On leave to England.	
RENINGHELST	24/12/15		Routine work - Conference with V.O.s of the Division.	
"	25/12/15		Routine work	
"	26/12/15		Routine work.	
"	27/12/15		Making arrangements with the Division for the testing of all animals with mallein. Malleined with Lieut PILKEY AVC 250 horses of the 1st Heavy Brigade R.G.A by intra dermal palpebral method. Heard late that the Division moving into rest area about 31st. Unable to [illegible] malleining of the Division.	
"	28/12/15		Inspecting 250 malleined horses - No reactions at 24th hour.	
"	29/12/15		Inspecting malleined horses & and malleining all the [illegible] not [illegible] for work. Could not complete owing to a call for [illegible] of ammunition [illegible] to the guns.	

1875 Wt. W593/826 1,000,000 4/15 J.B.C. & A. A.D.S.S./Forms/C. 2118.

Sheet N° 4

Instructions regarding War Diaries and Intelligence Summaries are contained in F. S. Regs., Part II. and the Staff Manual respectively. Title Pages will be prepared in manuscript.

WAR DIARY
~~or~~
~~INTELLIGENCE SUMMARY~~
(Erase heading not required.)

of Major W. W. R. Neale A.V.C. A.D.V.S. 17th Division

Army Form C. 2118

Place	Date	Hour	Summary of Events and Information	Remarks and references to Appendices
RENINGHELST	30/12/15		Inspecting malleined horses. Routine work. D.D.V.S. called.	
"	31/12/15		Inspecting malleined horses. No reactions. Conference with V.O's of the Division.	
			A very wet month. Ground always very muddy and waterlogged. Number of cases of Necrosis of the heels and pasterns largely increased. A few cases of Psoroptic mange but nothing serious.	
			W R Neale Major A.V.C. A.D.V.S. 17th Division	

1875 Wt. W593/826 1,000,000 4/15 J.B.C. & A. A.D.S.S./Forms/C. 2118.

A.D.M. 17th Div:
Vol: 7

Jan 1916

Sheet No 1

Instructions regarding War Diaries and Intelligence Summaries are contained in F. S. Regs., Part II. and the Staff Manual respectively. Title Pages will be prepared in manuscript.

WAR DIARY

~~or~~

~~INTELLIGENCE SUMMARY~~

(Erase heading not required.)

of Major W. W. R. Neale A.V.C.
A.D.V.S. 17th Division

Army Form C. 2118

Place	Date	Hour	Summary of Events and Information	Remarks and references to Appendices
RENINGHELST	1/1/16		Inspecting malleined horses of the 11th Heavy Brigade – No reactions –	
"	2/1/16		Malleined the horses of No 2 Entrenching Battalion – Routine work.	
"	3/1/16		Inspecting malleined horses of No 2 Entrenching Batt: No reaction at 24th hour – Received telegram from D.D.V.S. 2nd Army and letter from A.D.V.S. 24th Division saying our Mobile Section should be out of its present billet on the 8th inst. to allow the 24th Division Mobile Section in [illegible] the Divisions taking over from one another. As the move is spreading over 12 days arranged to leave Captain Howard Jones A.V.C. behind until the last of the Artillery moves.	
"	4/1/16		Issuing Remounts with the D.A.D.R.S. Inspecting malleined horses of No 2 Entrenching Batt. No reactions. Malleined the remaining eight horses of this unit.	
"	5/1/16		Visited malleined horses of No 2 Entrenching Batt: Proceeded to TILQUES to make arrangements for the move of No 29 Mobile Section.	
"	6/1/16		Visited malleined horses of No 2 Entrenching Batt: D.D.V.S. 2nd Army called whilst I was out. Later met him at No 29 Mobile Section.	
"	7/1/16		No 29 Mobile Section marched out on the way to new area at TILQUES.	

1875 Wt. W593/826 1,000,000 4/15 J.B.C. & A. A.D.S.S./Forms/C. 2118.

Sheet No 2

WAR DIARY
or
~~INTELLIGENCE~~ SUMMARY
(Erase heading not required.)

of Major W. W. R. Neale AVC
ADVS. 17th Division

Army Form C. 2118

Instructions regarding War Diaries and Intelligence Summaries are contained in F. S. Regs., Part II. and the Staff Manual respectively. Title Pages will be prepared in manuscript.

Place	Date	Hour	Summary of Events and Information	Remarks and references to Appendices
RENINGHELST	9/1/16		Moved from RENINGHELST to the rest area at TILQUES.	
TILQUES	9/1/16		Routine work.	
"	10/1/16		Proceeded to WULVERDINGHE to inspect a horse of the 81st Bde R.F.A. Amm: Col: left there sick on the march. Routine work.	
"	11/1/16		Proceeded to BONNINGUES to see a horse left in charge of the MAIRE by the 8/West Kent Regt. 24th Division. Routine work.	
"	12/1/16		Routine work.	
"	13/1/16		Routine work. The Division in this area is very scattered some of the Artillery units being 14 miles away from Headquarters. DDVS 2nd Army brought me a supply of Mallein Dilute and syringes for the testing of all animals of the Division. Lieut: J. S. G. KEPPEL A.V.C. No 29 Mobile Section went on leave.	
"	14/1/16		Routine work. Conference with V.O's of the Division. Work at Mobile Section.	
"	15/1/16		Routine work.	
"	16/1/16		Proceeded to JOURNY to inspect a horse left in charge of the MAIRE by the 108th Brigade R.F.A. 24th Division. Ordered it to be taken away by 81st Brigade R.F.A. Am: Col: until fit to travel to the Mobile Section.	

1875 Wt. W593/826 1,000,000 4/15 J.B.C. & A. A.D.S.S./Forms/C. 2118.

Sheet No. 3

WAR DIARY
or
INTELLIGENCE SUMMARY
(Erase heading not required.)

of Major W. W. R. Neale A.V.C. A.D.V.S. 17th Div.

Army Form C. 2118

Instructions regarding War Diaries and Intelligence Summaries are contained in F. S. Regs., Part II. and the Staff Manual respectively. Title Pages will be prepared in manuscript.

Place	Date	Hour	Summary of Events and Information	Remarks and references to Appendices
TILQUES	17/1/16		Routine work.	
"	18/1/16		Collecting two horses from Mons Joseph FLAVENT of ZUDAUSQUES which he had found. Routine work.	
"	19/1/16		Proceeded to OCHTEZEELE to inspect two horses left there sick by the 79th Brigade R.F.A. on the march. Routine work.	
"	20/1/16		Round various units of the Division with the DDR. and DAAMG. inspecting horses shown up for casting for other than Veterinary reasons.	
			Visited QUELMES to inspect a horse left there by the 24th Division	
"	21/1/16		Routine work.	
"	22/1/16		Routine work.	
"	23/1/16		Malleined in conjunction with Capt: A JACKSON, A.V.C three hundred and ninety two animals of the 78th Brigade R.F.A. Capt: KEPPEL A.V.C. returned from leave having been detained one day at FOLKESTONE and one day at BOULOGNE.	
"	24/1/16		Inspecting the malleined animals of 78th Brigade R.F.A	
"	25/1/16		Inspecting the malleining horses + mules of 78th Bde R.F.A. Malleined in conjunction with Capt: Jackson A.V.C. three hundred and forty five animals of	

Sheet No. 4

Instructions regarding War Diaries and Intelligence Summaries are contained in F. S. Regs., Part II. and the Staff Manual respectively. Title Pages will be prepared in manuscript.

WAR DIARY
or
~~INTELLIGENCE~~ SUMMARY

(Erase heading not required.)

of Major [illegible] A.V.C. A.D.V.S. 17th Division

Army Form C. 2118

Place	Date	Hour	Summary of Events and Information	Remarks and references to Appendices
TILQUES	25/1/16		of the 78th Bde R.F.A. this completing the Brigade.	
"	26/1/16		Inspecting malleined animals of 78th Bde R.F.A. – Inspecting sick horses left by the 9th Division at BOLLEZEELE and VOLKERINCKHOVE	
"	27/1/16		Inspecting malleined animals of 78th Bde R.F.A. – Malleining three hundred and thirty four animals of 79th Brigade R.F.A. in conjunction with Lieut. W. R. HILL, A.V.C. – Inspecting sick left by 9th Division at BROXEELE and LEDERZEELE	
"	28/1/16		Inspecting malleined animals of 79th Bde R.F.A. – Four hundred and twenty animals of 17th Div Amm. Col. malleined by Capt. KEPPEL A.V.C. and Lieut HILL A.V.C. – Capt KEPPEL in [illegible] had his hypodermic needle forced and broken off in the palm of his right hand.	
"	29/1/16		Inspecting malleined animals of 79th Bde R.F.A. – [illegible] animals of B. C and D Batteries 79th Bde R.F.A. – Inspecting malleined animals of 17th Div Amm. Col. – Lieut KEPPEL admitted to hospital [?]	

1875 Wt. W593/826 1,000,000 4/15 J.B.C. & A. A.D.S.S./Forms/C. 2118.

Sheet No 5

Instructions regarding War Diaries and Intelligence Summaries are contained in F. S. Regs., Part II. and the Staff Manual respectively. Title Pages will be prepared in manuscript.

WAR DIARY
or
~~INTELLIGENCE SUMMARY~~
(Erase heading not required.)

of Major W. W. R. Meade A.V.C.
A.D.V.S. 17th Div

Army Form C. 2118

Place	Date	Hour	Summary of Events and Information	Remarks and references to Appendices
TILQUES	30/1/16		Inspecting mallein'd animals of B.C. and D Batteries 79th Bde R.F.A. Six horses in B/79th Bde R.F.A. reactors at 20th hour – Informed D.D.V.S. 2nd Army by wire. Inspecting mallein'd animals of 17th Div Amn Col.	
"	31/1/16		Inspecting mallein'd animals of B.C. and D Batteries 79th Bde R.F.A. One more case reacted making a total of seven in B/79th Bde R.F.A. Destroyed and made a Post mortem examination of the seven reactors. D.D.V.S. 2nd Army present. P.M. Ex confirmed the accuracy of the test in every case.	
			W R Meade Major A.V.C. A.D.V.S. 17th Div	

1875 Wt. W593/826 1,000,000 4/15 J.B.C. & A. A.D.S.S./Forms/C. 2118.

A.D.V.S.

Hyd. Division

Vol VIII

Sheet No 1

Instructions regarding War Diaries and Intelligence Summaries are contained in F. S. Regs., Part II. and the Staff Manual respectively. Title Pages will be prepared in manuscript.

WAR DIARY
~~or~~
~~INTELLIGENCE SUMMARY~~
(Erase heading not required.)

of Major W.W.R. Neale AVC.
ADVS. 17th Division
B. E. F

Army Form C. 2118

Place	Date	Hour	Summary of Events and Information	Remarks and references to Appendices
TILQUES	1.2.16	.	Routine work and work in Mobile Section	
"	2.2.16		Malleinied 183 horses and 52 mules of 17th D.A.C. in conjunction with Lieut C HILL	
"	3.2.16		Inspecting Malleined animals of 17th D.A.C. - ordered to issue 116 ~~horses~~ Remounts to units at WATTEN. As a lot of units did not turn up it took the whole afternoon + evening which was time wasted.	
"	4.2.16		Inspecting Malleined animals of 17th D.A.C. No reactors. Work at 29 M.V.S	
"	5.2.16		Ordered to move the 29 Mobile Section at one hours notice and had 48 sick horses in some of which were unable to walk - Also left to find a new billet for the section. Found billet at ZUDUSQUES but had to leave the sick horses in a field at TILQUES as too late to move them. Very difficult as O.C. 29 M.V.S. still in hospital - Headquarters moved to TATINGHEM.	
TATINGHEM	6.2.16		Capt: KEPPEL O.C. 29 M.V.S. returned to duty from Hospital. Routine work	
"	7.2.16		Moved with Headquarters to RENINGHELST.	
RENINGHELST	8.2.16 } 9.2.16 }		Routine work.	

1875 Wt. W593/826 1,000,000 4/15 J.B.C. & A. A.D.S.S./Forms/C. 2118.

Sheet No 2.

WAR DIARY

~~or~~

~~INTELLIGENCE~~ SUMMARY

(Erase heading not required.)

of Major W.W.R. Neale AVC
ADVS. 17th Division
B.E.F.

Army Form C. 2118

Instructions [illegible] Diaries and Intelligence Summaries are contained in F. S. Regs., Part II. and the Staff Manual respectively. Title Pages will be prepared in manuscript.

Place	Date	Hour	Summary of Events and Information	Remarks and references to Appendices
RENINGHELST	10/2/16		Went back to ZUDAUSQUES to arrange the move of 29 M.V.S. and the collection of horses left behind by units.	
"	11.2.16		Had interview with the G.O.C re shortage of hay and no officers in the Artillery wagon lines when guns in action. Routine work.	
"	12.2.16		Taking over Heavy Draught horses from the 50th Division. Routine work.	
"	13/2/16 to 16/2/16	}	Routine work. Unable to mallein as all animals required for taking up ammunition &c.	
"	17/2/16		Malleined 109 Horses and 9 Mules of the Divisional Cavalry	
"	18/2/16		Inspecting malleined animals – Conference with V.O's of the Division	
"	19/2/16		Inspecting malleined animals – No reactors	
"	20/2/16 to 29/2/16	}	Malleining and inspecting malleined animals of units of the Division – Experimenting with the Thornton Forge in conjunction with A.D.V.S 24th Division	

W.R. Neale Major AVC
ADVS 17th Division

1875 Wt. W593/826 1,000,000 4/15 J.B.C. & A. A.D.S.S./Forms/C. 2118.

Sheet No. 1

WAR DIARY
or
~~INTELLIGENCE SUMMARY~~
(Erase heading not required.)

of Major W. W. R. Neale A.V.C. A.D.V.S. 17th Division

Army Form C. 2118

Instructions regarding War Diaries and Intelligence Summaries are contained in F. S. Regs., Part II. and the Staff Manual respectively. Title Pages will be prepared in manuscript.

Place	Date	Hour	Summary of Events and Information	Remarks and references to Appendices
RENINGHELST	1.3.16	.	Routine work. Malleinised all available horses (98) of 17th Divisional Train.	
"	2.3.16 to 4.3.16	}	Confined to bed with Laryngitis.	
"	5.3.16		Routine work. 78 Horses of 17th Divisional Train malleinised.	
"	6.3.16		Went to MERRIS to arrange for position of 29 M.V.S in the rest area. Inspecting malleinised horses.	
"	7.3.16		Headquarters of the Division moved to STEENVOORDE.	
STEENVOORDE	8.3.16 9.3.16	}	Routine work. D.D.V.S. called on 9th	
"	10.3.16		Headquarters of the Division moved to MERRIS.	
MERRIS	11.3.16 12.3.16 13.3.16 14.3.16	}	Routine work. D.D.V.S called on 13th & 14th	
"	15.3.16 to 22.3.16	}	Malleining horses and mules of 50th Inf: Bde 52nd Inf: Bde. C.R.E. and Yorkshire Dragoons and inspecting at 24th and 48th hours.	
"	23.3.16		Headquarters of the Division moved to ARMENTIERES.	
ARMENTIERES	24.3.16 to 31.3.16	}	Malleining animals of 51st 52nd 53rd Field Ambulances. 77. 78 and 93rd Field Coys R.E. 17th Div. Train and 51st Inf: Bde & inspecting them at 24th & 48th hours	

W.R. Neale Major A.V.C.
A.D.V.S. 17th Division

1875 Wt. W593/826 1,000,000 4/15 J.B.C. & A. A.D.S.S./Forms/C. 2118.

Sheet 1.

Instructions regarding War Diaries and Intelligence Summaries are contained in F. S. Regs., Part II. and the Staff Manual respectively. Title Pages will be prepared in manuscript.

WAR DIARY
~~or~~
~~INTELLIGENCE SUMMARY~~
(Erase heading not required.)

of Major W. W. R[illegible] ADVS. 17th Division

[illegible]y Form C. 2118

ADVS 17 Div

Place	Date	Hour	Summary of Events and Information	Remarks and references to Appendices
ARMENTIERES	1.4.16 to 4.4.16		Malleining and inspecting animals of 93rd Field Coy R.E., M.M.P., 78th Field Coy R.E. Headquarters 17th Division – On the 4th my horse slipped on the pavé road falling on me cutting my head open and injuring my elbow & hip – Captain R.N. WILLIAMS, A.V.C. arrived on the 4th vice Captain H.S. HOWARD-JONES A.V.C. invalided	10
"	5.4.16 & 6.4.16		Confined to bed by doctors orders.	
"	7.4.16		Resumed duty. Conference with V.O's of the Division	
"	8.4.16 to 11.4.16		Inspection duty.	
"	12.4.16 to 14.4.16		Malleining horses of 17th Divisional Cyclists and 1st Canadian Tunnelling Coy R.E. Routine work. Conference with V.O's of the Division	
"	15.4.16		Routine work.	
"	16.4.16 to 20.4.16		On Board of Inspection to enquire into the condition of animals of all units of the Division as ordered by Divisional Routine Order No 823 d/14/4/16 "B" Battery 79th Bde R.F.A. retested with mallein two reactors.	
"	21.4.16		Conference with V.O's of the Division	
"	22.4.16		Inspected horses of "B" Battery 80th Bde R.F.A. for mange	

1875 Wt. W593/826 1,000,000 4/15 J.B.C. & A. A.D.S.S./Forms/C. 2118.

Instructions regarding War Diaries and Intelligence Summaries are contained in F. S. Regs., Part II. and the Staff Manual respectively. Title Pages will be prepared in manuscript.

Sheet 2

WAR DIARY

or

~~INTELLIGENCE SUMMARY~~

(Erase heading not required.)

Of Major W. W. R. Ne[illegible] [illegible]
ADVS. 17th Division

Army Form C. 2118

Place	Date	Hour	Summary of Events and Information	Remarks and references to Appendices
ARMENTIERES	23.4.16		With DADRMG inspecting Remounts which arrived for the Division.	
"	24.4.16		Routine work.	
"	25.4.16		My clerk No 320 Cpl LINNELL, T. M., AVC evacuated sick suffering from Phthysis.	
"	26.4.16		Routine work.	
	27.4.16 to 30.4.16	}	On leave.	

W R Neale Major AVC
ADVS. 17th Division

1875 Wt. W593/826 1,000,000 4/15 J.B.C. & A. A.D.S.S./Forms/C. 2118.

Sheet No 1

Instructions regarding War Diaries and Intelligence Summaries are contained in F. S. Regs., Part II. and the Staff Manual respectively. Title Pages will be prepared in manuscript.

WAR DIARY
or
~~INTELLIGENCE SUMMARY~~
(Erase heading not required.)

of Major W. W. R. Neale A.V.C. A.D.V.S. 17th Division

Army Form C. 2118

VOL 11

Place	Date	Hour	Summary of Events and Information	Remarks and references to Appendices
	1/5/16 to 6/5/16		On short leave to England –	
ARMENTIERES	7/5/16		Inspecting animals at 29 M.V.S. for evacuation – Office work.	
"	8/5/16		Inspection duty – Requested to proceed to FLETRE to inspect and report on bulk forage some of which is reported unfit. Attended casting parade of D.D.R. 2nd Army	
"	9/5/16		Inspection duty – making enquiries re number of nails required per set of shoes as owing to scarcity it is proposed in the lighter shoes to cut the supply down from 60 per set to 40. Went to ESTAIRES to see the A.D.V.S. of the New Zealand Division which is to relieve us.	
"	10/5/16		"B" Battery 79th Brigade R.F.A. malleined for the 3rd time. Routine work.	
"	11/5/16		Showing A.D.V.S. New Zealand Division where all the wagon lines are and the M.V.S. Inspecting "B" Battery 80th Brigade R.F.A. with suspected skin disease – Owing to interchange of horses amongst Artillery units due to Brigade Ammunition Columns being done away with to avoid any of the animals going to other units I sent suspicious cases + his contacts to 29 M.V.S. for evacuation. Inspecting malleined horses.	

1875 Wt. W593/826 1,000,000 4/15 J.B.C. & A. A.D.S.S./Forms/C. 2118.

Sheet N° 2

Instructions regarding War Diaries and Intelligence Summaries are contained in F. S. Regs., Part II. and the Staff Manual respectively. Title Pages will be prepared in manuscript.

WAR DIARY
or
~~INTELLIGENCE SUMMARY~~

(Erase heading not required.)

of Major W. W. R. Meale AVC
ADVS 17th Division

Army Form C. 2118

Place	Date	Hour	Summary of Events and Information	Remarks and references to Appendices
ARMENTIERES	12/5/16		Inspecting horses of Brigade Ammunition Columns which are to be returned to Calais Remount Depôt. Found that the Batteries had sent their poor horses in and exchanged with the good horses of the Columns.	
"	13/5/16		Met DDR. 2nd Army to go through horses become surplus to the Division owing to reorganization of the Artillery.	
"	14/5/16		Routine work.	
"	15/5/16		Inspecting B/80th Bde R.F.A. for mange. Sent one suspicious case to M.V.S.	
"	16/5/16		Headquarters of the Division moved to TILQUES.	
TILQUES.	17/5/16		Inspection duty. Looking to see if could ~~get~~ get a more central position for 29 M.V.S.	
"	18/5/16		Inspection duty. Found 77th Field Coy R.E in a place very badly supplied with water. Advised "Q" to alter their billeting area.	
"	19/5/16 to 21/5/16		Inspecting duty.	
"	22/5/16		DDVS. 2nd Army inspected all units of 80th Brigade R.F.A. Mange found amongst the horses of B/80.	

1875 Wt. W593/826 1,000,000 4/15 J.B.C. & A. A.D.S.S./Forms/C. 2118.

Sheet No 3.

Instructions regarding War Diaries and Intelligence Summaries are contained in F. S. Regs., Part II. and the Staff Manual respectively. Title Pages will be prepared in manuscript.

WAR DIARY or INTELLIGENCE SUMMARY

of Major W W R Neale AVC. ADVS. 17th Division

(*Erase heading not required.*)

Army Form C. 2118

Place	Date	Hour	Summary of Events and Information	Remarks and references to Appendices
TILQUES	23/5/16		Inspecting units – Visited B/80th Bde R.F.A and gave instructions and made arrangements for the treatment of mange cases, disinfection of lines & all gear. Capt J J Keppel AVC OC 29 M.V.S. went on leave.	
"	24/5/16		Inspection duty	
"	25/5/16		Inspecting & giving instructions re the mange at B/80th Bde R.F.A.	
"	26/5/16		Inspection duty – No SS.762 Pte J. MACKIE. ASC joined as my clerk.	
"	27/5/16		Inspecting the 79th Bde R.F.A – No SE 14381 Pte F. PULHAM AVC transferred from clerk to line to 29 M.V.S.	
"	28/5/16 to 30/5/16		Inspection duty & visiting B/80th Bde R.F.A.	
"	31/5/16		Inspection duty – ADVS. 2nd Army inspected B/80th Bde R.F.A. and decided that one should be destroyed and 41 evacuated to the Base on 2nd prox. for mange.	
			W R Neale Major ADVS. 17th Division	

1875 Wt. W593/826 1,000,000 4/15 J.B.C. & A. A.D.S.S./Forms/C. 2118.

Sheet No 1

Instructions regarding War Diaries and Intelligence Summaries are contained in F. S. Regs., Part II. and the Staff Manual respectively. Title Pages will be prepared in manuscript.

WAR DIARY ~~or INTELLIGENCE SUMMARY~~ of Major W.W.R. Neale A.V.C. A.D.V.S. 17th Division

(Erase heading not required.)

Army Form C. 2118

Place	Date	Hour	Summary of Events and Information	Remarks and references to Appendices
TILQUES.	1.6.16		Interviewing C.R.A. with reference to mange outbreak in "B" Battery 80th Brigade R.F.A. Making arrangements for evacuating all the mange cases from B/80.	
"	2.6.16.		Inspection duty. All the horses of "B" Battery 79th Brigade R F A. malleined for the 4th time.	
"	3.6.16.		Routine work. Teaching new clerk how to do the weekly returns.	
"	4.6.16		Inspecting No 1 Company 17th Divisional Train at ESQUERDES.	
"	5.6.16		Inspecting Batteries. Visited by D.D.V.S. 2nd Army.	
"	6.6.16		Inspecting 17th D.A.C. at COULEMBY	
"	7.6.16.		Pte MACKIE A.S.C. sent up by my clerk under arrest for drunk, breaking arrest &c	
"	8.6.16		Office work Inspecting horses at 29 M.V.S.	
"	9.6.16		Inspecting newly joined Remounts with D.A.C. at COULEMBY reported by V.O. to be suspected mange cases. Pte Mackie A.S.C. my clerk awarded 28 days Field Punishment No 1 for 1 Drunkenness. 2 Breaking arrest 3. Threatening his superior officer	

1875 Wt. W593/826 1,000,000 4/15 J.B.C. & A. A.D.S.S./Forms/C. 2118.

Sheet No 2.

Instructions regarding War Diaries and Intelligence Summaries are contained in F. S. Regs., Part II. and the Staff Manual respectively. Title Pages will be prepared in manuscript.

WAR DIARY

~~or~~

~~INTELLIGENCE SUMMARY~~

(Erase heading not required.)

of Major W W R Neale A.V.C. ADVS. 17th Division

Army Form C. 2118

Vol 12

Place	Date	Hour	Summary of Events and Information	Remarks and references to Appendices
TILQUES.	10/6/16 11/6/16		Inspection duty	
"	12.6.16		Left the 2nd Army and proceeded to new area at ALLONVILLE. The 17th Division now part of the XVth Corps 4th Army.	
ALLONVILLE	13.6.16.		No 29 Mob: Vet: Section arrived in new area. Visiting Inspecting units DDVS. 4th Army called to see me.	
"	14.6.16 to 20.6.16		Inspecting units of the Division	
"	21.6.16		Went to XVth Corps Headquarters with DDVS. 4th Army with reference to a position for No 29 M.V.S. when we move up, where to put advanced collecting post &c.	
"	22.6.16 to 27.6.16		Inspecting units of the Division	
"	26.6.16		Moved with Headquarters of the Division from ALLONVILLE to MERICOURT	
MERICOURT	29.6.16		Inspection duty	
"	30.6.16		Part of the Headquarters moved to TREUX. I remained at MERICOURT. Conference with V.O's of the Division	

W W R Neale Major ADVS. 17th Division

1875 Wt. W593/826 1,000,000 4/15 J.B.C. & A. A.D.S.S./Forms/C. 2118.

Sheet No 1.

Instructions regarding War Diaries and Intelligence Summaries are contained in F. S. Regs., Part II. and the Staff Manual respectively. Title Pages will be prepared in manuscript.

WAR DIARY ~~or INTELLIGENCE SUMMARY~~

(Erase heading not required.)

of Major W. W. R. Neale A.V.C. ADVS. 17th Division

Army Form C. 2118

July

Vol 13

Place	Date	Hour	Summary of Events and Information	Remarks and references to Appendices
MERICOURT.	1.7.16 to 3.7.16		Inspection duty.	
"	4.7.16.		Headquarters moved from MERICOURT to VILLE. Took over the advanced Collecting station of No 33 M.V.S. 21st Division as the Collecting post for No 29 M.V.S.	
VILLE.	5.7.16 & 6.7.16		Inspection duty. Location of units very difficult to keep in touch with as they are constantly moving and are under the administration of different Divisions (7th & 21st)	
"	7.7.16		Inspection duty. Conference with V.O's of the Division	
"	8.7.16 to 10.7.16		Inspection duty.	
"	11.7.16		The Division with the exception of the Divisional Artillery move back to rest area & refit. Headquarters at CAVILLON. The Divisional Artillery remained in the line.	

1875 Wt. W593/826 1,000,000 4/15 J.B.C. & A. A.D.S.S./Forms/C. 2118.

Instructions regarding War Diaries and Intelligence Summaries are contained in F. S. Regs., Part II. and the Staff Manual respectively. Title Pages will be prepared in manuscript.

Sheet No 2

WAR DIARY
or
~~INTELLIGENCE SUMMARY~~
(Erase heading not required.)

of Major W. W. R. Neale AVC
ADVS. 17th Division

Army Form C. 2118

Place	Date	Hour	Summary of Events and Information	Remarks and references to Appendices
CAVILLON	12.7.16 to 14.7.16		Inspection duty	
"	15.7.16.		The Division less the Divisional Artillery and No 1 Company 17th Divisional Train moved to a new area. Headquarters at PONT REMY.	
PONT REMY	16.7.16 to 18.7.16		Inspection duty.	
"	19.7.16.		Captain J. J. G KEPPEL A.V.C. O.C. No 29 Mobile Veterinary Section admitted to Hospital with Tonsilitis – Inspection duty & work at M.V.S.	
"	20.7.16 & 21.7.16		Inspection duty and work at M.V.S.	
"	22.7.16		29 M.V.S. marched for new area with No 4 Group under an officer of 77th Field Coy R.E.	
"	23.7.16		Headquarters of the Division moved to RIBEMONT preparatory to the Division again going into the line –	
RIBEMONT	24.7.16		Routine work.	

1875 Wt. W593/826 1,000,000 4/15 J.B.C. & A. A.D.S.S./Forms/C. 2118.

Sheet No 3

Instructions regarding War Diaries and Intelligence Summaries are contained in F. S. Regs., Part II. and the Staff Manual respectively. Title Pages will be prepared in manuscript.

WAR DIARY

~~or~~

~~INTELLIGENCE SUMMARY~~

(*Erase heading not required.*)

of Major W. W. R. Neale AVC. ADVS. 17th Division

Army Form C. 2118

Place	Date	Hour	Summary of Events and Information	Remarks and references to Appendices
RIBEMONT	25.7.16 to 27.7.16	}	Inspecting all units of the Divisional Artillery. Found a large number of the horses very Debilitated and sent them to M.V.S. for evacuation. On investigation found the chief causes of emaciation to be insufficient & irregular watering and very long hours in draught.	
"	28.7.16		Conference with V.O's of the Division	
"	29.7.16 & 30.7.16	}	Inspection duty.	
"	31.7.16		Inspection duty. Captain J. J. G. KEPPEL A.V.C. O.C. 29 M.V.S. returned to duty from Hospital	

W R Neale Major
ADVS. 17th Division

1875 Wt. W593/826 1,000,000 4/15 J.B.C. & A. A.D.S.S./Forms/C. 2118.

Sheet N° 1

Instructions regarding War Diaries and Intelligence Summaries are contained in F. S. Regs., Part II. and the Staff Manual respectively. Title Pages will be prepared in manuscript.

WAR DIARY ~~or INTELLIGENCE SUMMARY~~ of Major W. W. R. Meale A.V.C. A.D.V.S. 17th Division

(Erase heading not required.)

Army Form C. 2118

Vol 14

Place	Date	Hour	Summary of Events and Information	Remarks and references to Appendices
RIBEMONT	1.8.16.		Visited A.D.V.S. 5th Division at BECORDEL to make arrangements on our Division taking over the line – The 5th Division M.V.S. not moving back but remaining up with their Artillery – made arrangements for 29 M.V.S. to have an advanced collecting post up but remainder of section to remain at Railhead –	
"	2.8.16.		Moved from RIBEMONT to ALBERT – wired O.C. 29 M.V.S. to establish a collecting post as early as possible at E11 d 7.6 map 62D N.E. and informed all V.O's of this.	
ALBERT	3.8.16.		Inspection duty.	
"	4.8.16.		Visiting collecting post – Conference with V.O's of the Division	
"	5.8.16.		Moved the office from the town of ALBERT to BELLEVUE FARM as ALBERT being shelled too much – Visited 29 M.V.S at RIBEMONT and inspected horses for evacuation.	
"	6.8.16.		Inspection duty.	
"	7.8.16.		Visiting collecting post and Capts: Henton – Hill – Williams and Sparling – with D.A.Q.M.G. viewing Remounts.	
"	8.8.16.		Inspection duty.	

1875 Wt. W593/826 1,000,000 4/15 J.B.C. & A. A.D.S.S./Forms/C. 2118.

Sheet No 2.

Instructions regarding War Diaries and Intelligence Summaries are contained in F. S. Regs., Part II. and the Staff Manual respectively. Title Pages will be prepared in manuscript.

WAR DIARY ~~or INTELLIGENCE SUMMARY~~

of Major W. W. R. Neale AVC A.D.V.S. 17th Division

(Erase heading not required.)

Army Form C. 2118

Place	Date	Hour	Summary of Events and Information	Remarks and references to Appendices
ALBERT.	9.8.16.		Issuing Remounts with D.A.A.M.G. - Inspected Remounts for suspected mange - Two very suspicious and had them isolated - Visited M.V.S and inspected animals for evacuation.	
"	10.8.16		Inspection duty	
"	11.8.16.		Inspection duty and conference with V.O's of the Division	
"	12.8.16.		Making arrangements for the move into the new area - Detailed Capt Sparling to march with the Infantry, R E Coys. &c and ordered Capt Heaton to take over the 81st I.A.B. from Capt Sparling	
"	13.8.16.		Moved from ALBERT to a camp situated between BUIRE and RIBEMONT (D 28 d 7.5 Map 62D NE.) The Infantry moving but Artillery remaining behind Handed over collecting post to 14th Division which relieving us. but ordered 29 M.V.S. to remain at RIBEMONT.	
Nr BUIRE	14.8.16.		Routine work.	
"	15.8.16		Moved to BERNAVILLE - All the Artillery & D.A.C. remaining behind - Gave orders to the M.V.S. to come on with the DAC when the Artillery rejoined the Division	

1875 Wt. W593/826 1,000,000 4/15 J.B.C. & A. A.D.S.S./Forms/C. 2118.

Sheet N°3.

Instructions regarding War Diaries and Intelligence Summaries are contained in F. S. Regs., Part II. and the Staff Manual respectively. Title Pages will be prepared in manuscript.

WAR DIARY of Major W. W. R. Neale AVC ADVS. 17th Division

~~or INTELLIGENCE SUMMARY~~

(Erase heading not required.)

Army Form C. 2118

Place	Date	Hour	Summary of Events and Information	Remarks and references to Appendices
BERNAVILLE	16.8.16		Moved from BERNAVILLE to DOULLENS and went on and interviewed ADVS. of the 56th Division from whom we are taking over and visited their M.V.S.	
DOULLENS.	17.8.16 to 20.8.16		Inspection duty + Routine work.	
"	21.8.16		Moved to new Headquarters at HENU	
HENU	22.8.16		Instructed by D.A.Q.M.G. to go to railhead (SAULTY- LARBRET) meet Remounts, detrain and issue them. Inspecting stables and giving instruction as to their disinfection.	
"	23.8.16		Inspection duty.	
"	24.8.16		Inspection duty. 29 M.V.S. moved up into new area and rejoined the Division. Billeted at GRINCOURT les PAS.	
"	25.8.16 to 29.8.16		Inspection duty	
"	30.8.16		Capt Henton A.V.C proceeded on 7 days special leave of absence to England.	

1875 Wt. W593/826 1,000,000 4/15 J.B.C. & A. A.D.S.S./Forms/C. 2118.

Sheet No 4

Instructions regarding War Diaries and Intelligence Summaries are contained in F. S. Regs., Part II. and the Staff Manual respectively. Title Pages will be prepared in manuscript.

WAR DIARY
or
~~INTELLIGENCE SUMMARY~~

(Erase heading not required.)

of Major W. W. R. Neale AVC
A.D.V.S. 17th Division

Army Form C. 2118

Place	Date	Hour	Summary of Events and Information	Remarks and references to Appendices
HENU	31/8/16.		Inspection duty – Mallein'd 15 horses of the North Irish Horse attached to M.M.P. 17th Division by order of D.D.V.S. Third Army as one of the N.I.H. horses evacuated by the 57th Division when tested at the base was found to be glandered –	

W.R. Neale Major
A.D.V.S. 17th Division

1875 Wt. W593/826 1,000,000 4/15 J.B.C. & A. A.D.S.S./Forms/C. 2118.

35

Confidential

WAR DIARY
SEPT 1916
of
A.D.V.S 17th DIVISION.

Sheet No 1.

Instructions regarding War Diaries and Intelligence Summaries are contained in F. S. Regs., Part II. and the Staff Manual respectively. Title Pages will be prepared in manuscript.

WAR DIARY

~~or~~

~~INTELLIGENCE SUMMARY~~

(Erase heading not required.)

of Major W.W.R. Neale AVC
ADVS. 17th Division

Army Form C. 2118

Place	Date	Hour	Summary of Events and Information	Remarks and references to Appendices
HENU	1.9.16		Inspecting a Mallenised horse of B/282 RFA 56th Division which had reacted. Ordered its destruction and made Post Mortem Exam: Nodules found in both lungs and left submaxillary gland enlarged and contained pus. Inspected No 1, 2 + 3 Sections of 17th DAC. Conference with V.O's of the Division.	
"	2.9.16		Making arrangements for putting field occupied by B/282 "Out of Bounds". Inspecting units and stable standings being erected for winter use.	
"	3.9.16		Routine work. DDVS. Third Army visited me.	
"	4.9.16		Routine work.	
"	5.9.16		Interview with AA + QMG. + DAQMG. re Veterinary matters in the Division. Forges in villages for use of units. Burial grounds for horses &c.	
"	6.9.16		Inspection duty. Capt. HENTON'S AVC leave extended on medical certificate to 12/9/16 Authority D.V.S. 3/2571/16 d/5/9/16. W.O. M3131/16 (V.D)	
"	7.9.16		Inspection duty.	
"	8.9.16		Inspecting 73 surplus horses of the Divisional Artillery on its re-organisation. Found it necessary to send 50 of these to the M.V.S. for evacuation. 2 suspected mange 1 lame and the remainder debilitated.	
"	9.9.16		Inspecting 10 further surplus horses of Divisional Artillery. Only 4 fit for re-issue remainder debilitated.	

1875 Wt. W593/826 1,000,000 4/15 J.B.C. & A. A.D.S.S./Forms/C. 2118.

Sheet No 2.

Instructions regarding War Diaries and Intelligence Summaries are contained in F. S. Regs., Part II. and the Staff Manual respectively. Title Pages will be prepared in manuscript.

WAR DIARY
or
INTELLIGENCE SUMMARY
(Erase heading not required.)

of Major W. W. R Neale A.V.C. D.D.V.S. 17th Division

Army Form C. 2118

Place	Date	Hour	Summary of Events and Information	Remarks and references to Appendices
HENU	10.9.16		Routine work.	
"	11.9.16		With D.D.V.S. Third Army who made an inspection of all units of the Divisional Artillery with the exception of the D.A.C.	
"	12.9.16		Inspection duty.	
"	13.9.16		Making arrangements for getting boxes for "NAILS" put up at all dumps & villages and getting the well where 78th Bde R.F.A. water deepened as it runs dry.	
"	14.9.16		Inspection duty.	
"	15.9.16		Sgt LEA RAY. BEVERIDGE and WINKLEY all A.V.C. who had become surplus owing to reorganisation of the Divisional Artillery reverted to unpaid acting Sergeants. Arrangements made for these N.C.O's to proceed to No 2 Veterinary Hospital – HAVRE on 16/9/16 – Conference with V.O's of the Division – Reported to D.D.V.S. Third Army that Captain HENTON A.V.C. not yet returned from sick leave.	
"	16.9.16		Routine work. Notified by VII Corps and D.D.V.S. Third Army (V132 d/15/9/16) that Capt: HENTON A.V.C. had been granted a further extension of leave on medical certificate to 25/9/16.	

1875 Wt. W593/826 1,000,000 4/15 J.B.C. & A. A.D.S.S./Forms/C. 2118.

Sheet No 3.

Instructions regarding War Diaries and Intelligence Summaries are contained in F. S. Regs., Part II. and the Staff Manual respectively. Title Pages will be prepared in manuscript.

WAR DIARY
or
INTELLIGENCE SUMMARY

of Major W. W. R. Neale AVC
A.D.V.S. 17th Division

(Erase heading not required.)

Army Form C. 2118

Place	Date	Hour	Summary of Events and Information	Remarks and references to Appendices
HENU	17.9.16		Inspection duty.	
"	18.9.16		Discussion at VII Corps Head Quarters with A.D.V.S. and A.D.V.S's of 33rd + 46th Division re "proposals for the prevention of Mange". Routine work.	
"	19.9.16 20.9.16		Inspection duty.	
"	21.9.16		On Board at 29 M.V.S. re horse of M DANICOURT of COUIN which had been run over by a lorry & was so severely injured that I ordered its destruction. Routine work. Seeing A.D.V.S. 33rd Division re taking over from me on the Division being relieved.	
"	22.9.16		Headquarters of the Division moved from HENU to ST RIQUIER. Lieut J. McR. FROST A.V.C reported his arrival for duty with the Division vice Capt F.K. HENTON AVC	
ST RIQUIER	23.9.16		Arranging farm billets &c for the Mobile Section.	
"	24.9.16 25.9.16		Inspection duty	
"	26.9.16		Conference with V.O's of the Division. Capt HENTON AVC rejoined the Division by orders of the D.V.S. and Lieut FROST AVC posted to 21st Division	

1875 Wt. W593/826 1,000,000 4/15 J.B.C. & A. A.D.S.S./Forms/C. 2118.

Sheet No 4.

Instructions regarding War Diaries and Intelligence Summaries are contained in F. S. Regs., Part II. and the Staff Manual respectively. Title Pages will be prepared in manuscript.

WAR DIARY
or
INTELLIGENCE SUMMARY
(Erase heading not required.)

of Major W. W. R. Neale A.V.C. A.D.V.S. 17th Division

Army Form C. 2118

Place	Date	Hour	Summary of Events and Information	Remarks and references to Appendices
ST RIQUIER	27.9.16 to 30.9.16	}	Inspecting units of the Division	

W. R. Neale Major
A.D.V.S. 17th Division

1875 Wt. W593/826 1,000,000 4/15 J.B.C. & A. A.D.S.S./Forms/C. 2118.

CONFIDENTIAL

Vol 16

WAR DIARY

of

A.D.V.S. 17 DIVISION

FOR

October 1916.

Instructions regarding War Diaries and Intelligence Summaries are contained in F. S. Regs., Part II. and the Staff Manual respectively. Title Pages will be prepared in manuscript.

WAR DIARY or ~~INTELLIGENCE SUMMARY~~

(Erase heading not required.)

Army Form C. 2118.

Sheet No. 1 — of Major W. W. R. Neale A.V.C. A.D.V.S. 17th Division

Place	Date	Hour	Summary of Events and Information	Remarks and references to Appendices
ST RIQUIER	1-10-16.		Received instructions to direct Capt: P. S. SPARLING A.V.C. to proceed to the 15th Division vice Capt: V. W. F. WALKER, A.V.C. Also that Capt SPARLING would be relieved by Lieut: P. W. WALKER AVC. (T.C) - Inspection duty -	
"	2.10.16		Visited Capt: SPARLING at PAS where the Divisional Artillery are in camp & gave him instructions not to leave the Division until Lieut: WALKER had arrived and he had handed over to him - Inspecting 81st Bde R.F.A.	
"	3.10.16		Issued wallets Veterinary Mark IV one to each M. G. Coy: as authorised by D.V.S. through D.D.V.S. Third Army. Inspection duty.	
"	4.10.16		Duty concerning Remounts being drawn by 29 M.V.S. for the Division. Routine work.	
"	5.10.16		Inspection duty with D.A.C. at PAS HUTS - Orders received for 29 M.V.S. to march with 50th Inf: Bde tomorrow to forward area. Wired to No. 12 Vety Hospl to know when I might expect the arrival of Lieut P. W. WALKER. Received reply that he had no instructions re Lieut WALKER. Informed D.D.V.S. Third Army.	
"	6.10.16		Headquarters moved from ST RIQUIER to PAS.	
PAS.	7.10.16.		At "Q" to find out where 29 M.V.S. was to be located - Told HURTEBISE FARM	

2449 Wt. W14957/M90 750,000 1/16 J.B.C. & A. Forms/C.2118/12.

Instructions regarding War Diaries and Intelligence Summaries are contained in F. S. Regs., Part II. and the Staff Manual respectively. Title Pages will be prepared in manuscript.

Sheet No 2

WAR DIARY
or
INTELLIGENCE SUMMARY
(Erase heading not required.)

of Major W. W. R. Neale A.V.C. A.D.V.S. 17th Division

Army Form C. 2118.

Place	Date	Hour	Summary of Events and Information	Remarks and references to Appendices
PAS	7.10.16		Went there to make arrangements and found it in possession of the 33rd Division Gas school. Later informed that could not go there as the Divisional area had been changed.	
"	8.10.16		Was told to find a site for the Mobile section myself. Very difficult as all available ground already taken up. Eventually selected a piece of ground and got the permission of the Town Major. PAS HUTS to put the M.V.S. there	
"	9.10.16		Routine work. 29 M.V.S. marched in.	
"	10.10.16		Inspection duty. Lieut R. W. WARNER, A.V.C. (T.C.) joined the Division and Captain R. S. SPARLING, A.V.C. left it to join the 15th Division.	
"	11.10.16 & 12.10.16		Inspection duty.	
"	13.10.16		Conference with V.O's of the Division. Visited D.D.V.S. Third Army at Army Headquarters. St POL re Captain F. R. HENTON A.V.C. (T.C.) owing to a report having been made concerning this Officer's behaviour at mess by O.C. No 4 Company 17th Divisional Train	

2449 Wt. W14957/M90 750,000 1/16 J.B.C. & A. Forms/C.2118/12.

Army Form C. 2118.

Instructions regarding War Diaries and Intelligence Summaries are contained in F. S. Regs., Part II. and the Staff Manual respectively. Title Pages will be prepared in manuscript.

Sheet No 3.

WAR DIARY or ~~INTELLIGENCE SUMMARY~~

(Erase heading not required.)

of Major W. W. R. Neale A.V.C. A.D.V.S. 17th Division

Place	Date	Hour	Summary of Events and Information	Remarks and references to Appendices
PAS.	14.10.16		D.D.V.S. Third Army visited and had interview with Captain F. R. HENTON, A.V.C. (T.C.) re the complaint against him – Afterwards the D.D.V.S. Third Army inspected the 17th D.A.C. and 17th Divisional Train.	
"	15.10.16		Routine work. Forwarded subscriptions of A.V.C. personnel exclusive of 29 M.V.S. for the Lord Kitchener Memorial Fund to D.D.V.S. Third Army.	
"	16.10.16		Inspection duty – Ordered 23 debility cases from 78th Bde R.F.A. to the M.V.S. Captain W. R. HILL A.V.C. (T.C.) granted short leave of absence to U.K.	
"	17.10.16		Inspection duty.	
"	18.10.16		The Divisional Artillery left the area for SENLIS. Routine work.	
"	19.10.16		Inspection duty.	
"	20.10.16		Went to BAZIEUX re move of the Division into 3rd Corps – On arrival there found that the move had been altered & that the Division was to go to the Fourth Army – Went on to MEAULTE to see where M.V.S. to be located re.	
"	21.10.16		Division on the move – Gave instructions to O.C. 29 M.V.S. re the move of the section tomorrow.	

2449 Wt. W14957/M90 750,000 1/16 J.B.C. & A. Forms/C.2118/12.

Instructions regarding War Diaries and Intelligence Summaries are contained in F. S. Regs., Part II. and the Staff Manual respectively. Title Pages will be prepared in manuscript.

Sheet No 4

WAR DIARY
or
INTELLIGENCE SUMMARY

(Erase heading not required.)

of Major W.W.R. Neale AVC
ADVS. 17th Division

Army Form C. 2118.

Place	Date	Hour	Summary of Events and Information	Remarks and references to Appendices
PAS	22.10.16		Headquarters moved from PAS to TREUX – left Third Army & joined Fourth Army.	
TREUX	23.10.16		Inspection duty at MERICOURT and VILLE.	
"	24.10.16		DDVS Fourth Army visited the Division particularly with regard to No 3374 P/A/Sergt BATT. J. AVC. whom I had reported to DDVS Third Army as both inefficient and negligent.	
"	25.10.16		Inspection duty.	
"	26.10.16		Visited 17th DAC and the Divisional Artillery wagon lines now in the Reserve Army. Found P/A/Sgt BATT AVC had been admitted to Hospital so was ~~[illegible]~~ unable to comply with DDVS Fourth Army instructions contained in his letter No 1802 d/24/10/16 V23 to revert the NCO to his permanent grade & send him to No 2 Veterinary Hospital.	
"	27.10.16		Headquarters left TREUX and went forward into camp at the BRIDGE on the FRICOURT – BRAY Road. Capt N.R HILL AVC (T.C) resumed duty from leave of absence to UK. No 24 Mobile Veterinary Section moved to MEAULTE.	

2449 Wt. W14957/M90 750,000 1/16 J.B.C. & A. Forms/C.2118/12.

Instructions regarding War Diaries and Intelligence Summaries are contained in F. S. Regs., Part II. and the Staff Manual respectively. Title Pages will be prepared in manuscript.

Sheet No 5.

WAR DIARY
or
INTELLIGENCE SUMMARY
(Erase heading not required.)

of Major W.W.R. Neale A.V.C.
A.D.V.S. 17th Division

Army Form C. 2118.

Place	Date	Hour	Summary of Events and Information	Remarks and references to Appendices
CITADEL	28/10/16		Routine work – Conference with the V.O's of the Division –	
"	29/10/16		Inspection duty – Visited A.D.V.S. 8th Division re taking over when our Division relieves them –	
"	30/10/16		Routine work.	
"	31.10.16		Headquarters moved from the CITADEL to MINDEN POST (between FRICOURT and MARICOURT) and 29 M.V.S. moved to A19 B6.6. (Albert Combined Sheet) 2 Kilometres W of MARICOURT.	

W.R. Neale Major
A.D.V.S. 17th Division

2449 Wt. W14957/M90 750,000 1/16 J.B.C. & A. Forms/C.2118/12.

WAR DIARY

ADVS, 17 DIVN

&

29th Mob Vet Section

for

NOVEMBER 1916

Vol 17

Instructions regarding War Diaries and Intelligence Summaries are contained in F. S. Regs., Part II. and the Staff Manual respectively. Title Pages will be prepared in manuscript.

Sheet No 1.

WAR DIARY ~~or~~ ~~INTELLIGENCE SUMMARY~~

(*Erase heading not required.*)

of Major W.W.R. Meale A.V.C.
A.D.V.S. 17th Division

Army Form C. 2118.

Place	Date	Hour	Summary of Events and Information	Remarks and references to Appendices
MINDEN POST	1/11/16.		Endeavouring to get a suitable place for 29 M.V.S. – At present it is out in the open in deep mud without any shelter for the personnel, forage or equipment – C.R.E. unable to give any material to make cover – Men had to take shelter for the night in the forage shelter of the 8th Divn M.V.S.	
"	2/11/16.		No other site available for the M.V.S. but got tents for the personnel &c. Inspected the Infantry Brigades transport animals. Conditions of the lines could not be worse, mud very deep and exceedingly sticky – Large numbers of shoes are pulled off by the holding mud daily, breaking the feet badly and causing a lot of lameness.	
"	3/11/16		Routine work – Conference with V.O's. of the 6th Divisional Artillery which is under my administration.	
"	4/11/16		Visited the 17th Divisional Artillery which is attached to 19th Division for administration and met the A.D.V.S. 19th Division – Visited all V.O's of the 17th Divn Artillery.	
"	5/11/16 + 6/11/16.		Inspecting ~~wag~~ transport animals of Field Ambulance and advanced Headquarters.	

2449 Wt. W14957/M90 750,000 1/16 J.B.C. & A. Forms/C.2118/12.

Instructions regarding War Diaries and Intelligence Summaries are contained in F. S. Regs., Part II. and the Staff Manual respectively. Title Pages will be prepared in manuscript.

Sheet No 2.

WAR DIARY
or
INTELLIGENCE SUMMARY
(Erase heading not required.)

of Major W. W. R. Neale AVC. ADVS. 17th Division

Army Form C. 2118.

Place	Date	Hour	Summary of Events and Information	Remarks and references to Appendices
MINDEN POST	7/11/16.		Under instructions from DDVS. 4th Army inspected XIV Corps Heavy Artillery and went into the watering arrangements particularly and the stable management generally. Conditions extremely bad - Lines in deep holding mud - water troughs between 2 & 3 miles away through such mud as to leave the horses exhausted after the journey - Owing to distance to water and also to the gun position horses out from 18 to 24 hours - A large number of the horses very debilitated owing to the conditions and also to the Batteries being very short of horses. - For the latter reason & also because only half loads could be taken to the guns at a time horses were doing double journeys - Report on all these conditions forwarded to DDVS. 4th Army on 8/11/16.	
"	8/11/16 - 9/11/16		Inspecting 17th Divisional units.	
"	10/11/16		Under instructions from DDVS. Fourth Army inspected the 12th. 124th 159th 181st. 158th and 1/1 Lancs Heavy Batteries - A large number of the animals very debilitated owing to the conditions under which they are living, hard work through deep and holding mud, number of hours they have to be at work, long distances they have to travel to water and short hay ration which has recently been reduced from 15 lbs to 8 lbs per diem.	
"	11/11/16		Routine work.	

2449 Wt. W14957/M90 750,000 1/16 J.B.C. & A. Forms/C.2118/12.

Army Form C. 2118.

Instructions regarding War Diaries and Intelligence Summaries are contained in F. S. Regs., Part II. and the Staff Manual respectively. Title Pages will be prepared in manuscript.

Sheet No 3.

WAR DIARY
or
~~INTELLIGENCE SUMMARY~~

(*Erase heading not required.*)

of Major W. W. P. Mears A.V.C.
A.D.V.S. 17th Division

Place	Date	Hour	Summary of Events and Information	Remarks and references to Appendices
MINDEN POST	12/11/16		D.D.V.S. 4th Army came and together we visited 29 M.V.S. 15 M.V.S. and 46 M.V.S. discussing matters concerning evacuation of the large number of sick animals &c.	
"	13/11/16		Inspection duty.	
"	14/11/16		Inspection duty. Headquarters moved from MINDEN POST to TREUX.	
TREUX	15/11/16		Headquarters moved from TREUX to CAVILLON (rest area)	
CAVILLON	16/11/16		Inspection duty. 29 M.V.S. marched in to OISSY (rest area)	
"	17/11/16		Routine work.	
"	18/11/16			
	19/11/16 to 28/11/16		On leave of absence to England. O.C. 29 M.V.S (Capt: J. J. G. Keppel A.V.C.) officiating for me	
	29/11/16 30/11/16		Returning from leave. Detained in Boulogne one night.	
			- Remarks -	
			During this month the hay ration was reduced to 8 lbs per animal per diem.	
			Number of cases of "picked up nail" in the forward area very large.	
			Number of cases of "Necrotic ulcer" very much on the increase.	
			Watering of animals in the forward area very difficult owing to the comparatively few water places & the journey through mud.	
			Large number of shoes pulled off by the mud.	

2449 Wt. W14957/M90 750,000 1/16 J.B.C. & A. Forms/C.2118/12.

Sheet No 4

Army Form C. 2118.

WAR DIARY
or
~~INTELLIGENCE SUMMARY~~

(Erase heading not required.)

of Major W. W. R. Meale AVC.
ADVS. 17th Division

Instructions regarding War Diaries and Intelligence Summaries are contained in F. S. Regs., Part II. and the Staff Manual respectively. Title Pages will be prepared in manuscript.

Place	Date	Hour	Summary of Events and Information	Remarks and references to Appendices
In the Field			Remarks (Continued) Owing to the large number of animals requiring evacuation in the forward area the personnel of the M.V.S was insufficient to deal with them and supply conducting parties by rail. A large proportion of the sick animals came from Corps troops and these having no M.V.S. have to be cleared by Divisional M.V.S's W. R. Meale Major AVC. ADVS. 17th Division	

2449 Wt. W14957/M90 750,000 1/16 J.B.C. & A. Forms/C.2118/12.

Army Form C. 2118.

WAR DIARY
or
INTELLIGENCE SUMMARY
(*Erase heading not required.*)

Instructions regarding War Diaries and Intelligence Summaries are contained in F. S. Regs., Part II. and the Staff Manual respectively. Title Pages will be prepared in manuscript.

Sheet No 1

of Major W. W. R. [illegible] A.V.C.
A.D.V.S. 17th Division

Vol 18

Place	Date	Hour	Summary of Events and Information	Remarks and references to Appendices
CAVILLON	1/12/16 to 3/12/16		Inspecting the 50th 51st + 52nd Infantry Brigades. 31st + 115th Heavy Batteries R.G.A. (XIV Corps) A + B Batteries 74th Brigade R.F.A. Guards Division and No 3 Section Guards D.A.C.	
"	4/12/16		Routine work. Sergt. SANDFORD A.V.C. joined the Division for duty with the 81st Brigade R.F.A.	
"	5/12/16		Routine work.	
"	6/12/16		Inspection duty. Delivered a Veterinary lecture to the 52nd Infantry Bde at AILLY SUR SOMME.	
"	7/12/16		Routine work. Delivered a Veterinary lecture to the 50th Infantry Bde at MOLLIENS VIDAME. Capt: J. J. G. KEPPEL A.V.C. O.C. 29 M.V.S. Procured on leave.	
"	8/12/16		Routine work. Delivered a Veterinary lecture to the 51st Infantry Brigade at PICQUIGNY. Carrying on duties of O.C. 29 M.V.S.	
"	9/12/16		Visited 29 M.V.S. + inspected horses for evacuation. Inspection duty.	

2449 Wt. W14957/M90 750,000 1/16 J.B.C. & A. Forms/C.2118/12.

Instructions regarding War Diaries and Intelligence Summaries are contained in F. S. Regs., Part II. and the Staff Manual respectively. Title Pages will be prepared in manuscript.

Sheet No. 2

WAR DIARY or INTELLIGENCE SUMMARY

(Erase heading not required.)

of Major W. W. R. Neale AVC. ADVS. 17th Division

Army Form C. 2118.

Place	Date	Hour	Summary of Events and Information	Remarks and references to Appendices
CAVILLON	10/12/16		Evacuating sick from M.V.S. – Visiting inhabitants at DREUIL LES MOLLIENS and CLAIRY SAULCHOIX reported to have Government horses in their possession with a view to identification & collection.	
"	11/12/16 + 12/12/16		Work at 29 M.V.S. – Inspection duty – Making arrangements for the horses of the Division.	
"	13/12/16		Headquarters & 29 M.V.S. moved to CORBIE.	
CORBIE	14/12/16		Getting more suitable stabling & lines for 29 M.V.S. The stabling & lines occupied by the outgoing M.V.S. had been handed over to Infantry Transport by the Town Major.	
"	15/12/16		Inspection duty – Collecting sick & lame animals left behind by units of other Division	
"	16/12/16		Inspection duty & collecting sick.	
"	17/12/16		Inspecting 26th Heavy Battery R.G.A. ANZAC Corps. & 53rd Field Ambulance	
"	18/12/16 to 24/12/16		Inspection duty – Collecting & evacuating sick animals.	

2449 Wt. W14957/M90 750,000 1/16 J.B.C. & A. Forms/C.2118/12.

Shut No 3

Army Form C. 2118.

Instructions regarding War Diaries and Intelligence Summaries are contained in F. S. Regs., Part II. and the Staff Manual respectively. Title Pages will be prepared in manuscript.

WAR DIARY or INTELLIGENCE SUMMARY

(Erase heading not required.)

of Major W.R. Neale A.V.C.
A.D.V.S. 17th Division

Vol

Place	Date	Hour	Summary of Events and Information	Remarks and references to Appendices
CORBIE.	21/12/16		Inspection duty - Found two cases of mange at 51st Field Ambulance - Received notification that Capt J.F.G. KEPPEL A.V.C. OC 29 M.V.S. had been granted extension of leave on medical certificate until Dec 28th 1916 (Authority D.D.V.S. Fourth Army No 2111 d/20/12/16. D.V.S. No 3/463/16 d/20/12/16)	
"	22/12/16		Routine work.	
"	23/12/16		Attended conference at Office of D.D.V.S. Fourth Army. Routine work.	
"	24/12/16		Placed Captain F.K. HENTON A.V.C. in charge of 29 M.V.S. until Capt KEPPEL A.V.C returns from extended leave on medical certificate	
"	25/12/16		Headquarters moved to forward area A2d 9.7 ALBERT (Combined sheet) and 29 M.V.S. to F17b 5.3 ALBERT (Combined sheet)	
In the Field	26/12/16 to 31/12/16		Inspection duty. Inspection duty - Found 2 cases of mange in the 78th Field Coy R.E. and an outbreak (9 cases) in "C" Battery 78th Brigade R.F.A. Reported to D.D.V.S Fourth Army.	

W.R. Neale Major A.V.C.
A.D.V.S. 17th Div.

2449 Wt. W14957/M90 750,000 1/16 J.B.C. & A. Forms/C.2118/12.

Instructions regarding War Diaries and Intelligence Summaries are contained in F. S. Regs., Part II. and the Staff Manual respectively. Title pages will be prepared in manuscript.

Sheet No 1

WAR DIARY
or
~~INTELLIGENCE SUMMARY.~~

(Erase heading not required.)

of Major W. W. Rhead (?) A.V.C.
ADVS 17th Division

Vol 19

Army Form C. 2118.

Place	Date	Hour	Summary of Events and Information	Remarks and references to Appendices
A2d47 ALBERT (Combined Sheet)	1/1/17		Routine work. Received XIV Corps No A/6202 notifying me that Captain KEPPEL'S AVC, SR / OC 29 Mobile Veterinary Section has been extended to 31/1/17 on medical certificate.	
"	2/1/17		Inspection duty.	
"	3/1/17		Inspection duty. Found an outbreak of Mange in "C" Battery 78th Brigade RFA in rest area at MORLANCOURT. Informed DDVS and 2nd and evacuated the diseased animals, segregated in contacts, gave orders for disinfection of all gear and arranged separate water troughs for the Battery.	
"	4/1/17		Inspection duty	
"	5/1/17		Inspection duty. Conference with the VOs of the Division	
"	6/1/17		Routine work.	
"	7/1/17		Captain T.J.G. KEPPEL AVC (SR) returned from extended leave on medical certificate.	

A5834 Wt. W4973/M687 750,000 8/16 D. D. & L. Ltd. Forms/C.2118/13.

Sheet No 2.

Instructions regarding War Diaries and Intelligence Summaries are contained in F. S. Regs., Part II. and the Staff Manual respectively. Title pages will be prepared in manuscript.

WAR DIARY
or
INTELLIGENCE SUMMARY.
(*Erase heading not required.*)

of Major W. W. R. Neale A.V.C.
A.D.V.S. 17th Division

Army Form C. 2118.

Place	Date	Hour	Summary of Events and Information	Remarks and references to Appendices
A2d 9.7 ALBERT (Combined Sheet)	9/1/17 to 10/1/17		Inspection duty.	
"	11/1/17		Routine work. Captain H. N. M. WILLIAMS A.V.C. (T.C.) proceeded on leave.	
"	12/1/17		Inspection duty. Under instructions from D.V.S through D.D.V.S. Fourth Army reverted No S.E. 2923 P/A/Sergt SANDFORD A.V.C. to his permanent rank on account of ill health and gave instructions for his return to No 2 Veterinary Hospital.	
"	13/1/17		Inspection duty. Posted No S E 3068 P/A/Sergt WILLIS A.V.C. to the 78th Brigade R.F.A. vice P/A/Sergt SANDFORD A.V.C. – Sergt WILLIS became surplus owing to re-organization of the Artillery. The 81st Brigade R.F.A. being broken up.	
"	14/1/17		Inspection duty.	
"	15/1/17		Routine work.	

A5834 Wt. W4973/M687 750,000 8/16 D. D. & L. Ltd. Forms/C.2118/13.

Sheet No 3

Instructions regarding War Diaries and Intelligence Summaries are contained in F. S. Regs., Part II. and the Staff Manual respectively. Title pages will be prepared in manuscript.

WAR DIARY
or
INTELLIGENCE SUMMARY.
(*Erase heading not required.*)

of Major W. W. R. Neale AVC
ADVS 17th Division

Army Form C. 2118.

Place	Date	Hour	Summary of Events and Information	Remarks and references to Appendices
In the Field	16/1/17		Moved with Divisional Headquarters from forward area to the rest area at CORBIE. 29 M.V.S. also moved to CORBIE.	
CORBIE	17/1/17 to 19/1/17		Inspection duty & Routine work.	
"	20/1/17		Attended Conference of ADsVS. at office of DDVS. Fourth Army.	
"	21/1/17 to 22/1/17		Inspection duty	
"	23/1/17		Inspection duty. Found seven very slight cases of Contagious Stomatitis in the horses of 93rd Field Coy RE	
"	24/1/17		Inspection duty. Col KENDALL [illegible] AVC from the office of DDVS Fourth Army called re the Contagious Stomatitis in 93rd Field Coy R.E.	
"	25/1/17		Went with DDVS. Fourth Army to inspect the Contagious Stomatitis cases	
"	26/1/17		Routine work. Inspecting & receiving Remounts at EDGEHILL Siding	

A5834 Wt. W4973/M687 750,000 8/16 D. D. & L. Ltd. Forms/C.2118/13.

Sheet No 4

Instructions regarding War Diaries and Intelligence Summaries are contained in F. S. Regs., Part II. and the Staff Manual respectively. Title pages will be prepared in manuscript.

WAR DIARY or INTELLIGENCE SUMMARY.

(Erase heading not required.)

of Major W. R. Meale A.V.C. A.D.V.S. 17th Division

Army Form C. 2118.

Place	Date	Hour	Summary of Events and Information	Remarks and references to Appendices
In the Field	28/1/17		Moved with Divisional Headquarters from CORBIE to the forward area F17d62 (MINDEN POST). – Orders that no sick horses be evacuated until further orders. 29 M.V.S. moved up on 27/1/17.	
"	29/1/17 } 30/1/17		Inspection duty. Several cases of Mange in the 78th Brigade R.F.A. "B and C" Batteries.	
"	31/1/17		Inspection duty. Thirteen cases of Contagious Stomatitis in "C" Battery 78th Brigade R.F.A. Attended conference of A.D.V.S. at Office of D.D.V.S. Fourth Army.	
			During the last ten days of this month there was some snow and very severe frost.	
			W. R. Meale Major A.V.C. A.D.V.S. 17th Division	

A5834 Wt. W4973/M687 750,000 8/16 D. D. & L. Ltd. Forms/C.2118/13.

Vol 20

Confidential

War Diary

of

A.D.V.S. (Major W.W.R. NEALE A.V.C.) 17th Divn

and

~~29th Mobile Veterinary~~ Sect.

A.V.C.

att

17th Division

for

February 1919

Sheet No 1

Instructions regarding War Diaries and Intelligence Summaries are contained in F. S. Regs., Part II. and the Staff Manual respectively. Title pages will be prepared in manuscript.

WAR DIARY ~~or~~ ~~INTELLIGENCE SUMMARY.~~

(*Erase heading not required.*)

of Major W. W. R. Neale A.V.C. A.D.V.S. 17th Division

Army Form C. 2118.

Place	Date	Hour	Summary of Events and Information	Remarks and references to Appendices
In the Field F18C3.3 ALBERT (Combined Sheet)	1/2/17 to 5/2/17		Inspection duty - Cases of Stomatitis still occurring but not in large numbers. Mange however very much on the increase - variety Sarcoptic, chiefly attacking the head and neck -	
"	6/2/17		Thirty two animals of the 17th D.A.C. Killed or so badly injured that they had to be destroyed and 27 wounded, also 3 wounded in C/78 Bde R.F.A by a bomb dropped from a hostile aeroplane. Captain C. Nicholson A.V.C. joined the Division for duty vice Captain R.N.W. Williams A.V.C. who was taken ill whilst on leave to the U.K.	
"	7/2/17		D.D.V.S. Fourth Army came and inspected the Mange Cases of 78th Bde. RFA with me and the V.O. i/c (Capt: A. Jackson A.V.C.) I had reported the increase of Mange and not being allowed to evacuate them to the L of C owing to prevalence of Stomatitis Contagiosa had suggested forming a Mange Camp in the Reserve or Rest area. Given instructions to treat in the unit -	
"	8/2/17 to 13/2/17		Inspection duty - On the 9/2/17 held a conference with V.O's of the Division	

A5834 Wt. W4973/M687 750,000 8/16 D. D. & L. Ltd. Forms/C.2118/13.

Sheet No 2.

Instructions regarding War Diaries and Intelligence Summaries are contained in F. S. Regs., Part II. and the Staff Manual respectively. Title pages will be prepared in manuscript.

WAR DIARY ~~or INTELLIGENCE SUMMARY~~.

(*Erase heading not required.*)

of Major W.S. [illegible] A.V.C. A.D.V.S 17th Division

Army Form C. 2118.

Place	Date	Hour	Summary of Events and Information	Remarks and references to Appendices
In the Field F.I.F.C.3.3 ALBERT (Combined sheet)	14/2/17		Attended conference of A.D's V.S at office of D.D.V.S. Fourth Army.	
	15/2/17		Inspection duty	
"	16/2/17		Conference with V.O's of the Division - Captain F.K. HENTON A.V.C. (T.C) left the Division and joined the 61st Division for temporary duty - Authority D.D.V.S. No 127 d/13/2/17 and 17th Division wire A/115 dated 14/2/17.	
"	17/2/17		Routine work.	
"	18/2/17		Thaw set in - Up to this day during the whole of the month there was severe frost rendering watering arrangements extremely difficult owing to the troughs & pipes freezing every night -	
"	19/2/17		D.D.V.S. Fourth Army visited me and gave instructions what to do with Contagious Stomatitis cases if the Division leaves the Fourth Army.	
"	20/2/17		Routine work.	

A5834 Wt. W4973/M687 750,000 8/16 D. D. & L. Ltd. Forms/C.2118/13.

Sheet No 3.

Instructions regarding War Diaries and Intelligence Summaries are contained in F. S. Regs., Part II. and the Staff Manual respectively. Title pages will be prepared in manuscript.

WAR DIARY or ~~INTELLIGENCE SUMMARY~~.

(Erase heading not required.)

of Major W. W. R. Neale AVC. ADVS. 17th Division

Army Form C. 2118.

Place	Date	Hour	Summary of Events and Information	Remarks and references to Appendices
In the Field	21/2/17		Inspection duty. Headquarters of the Division and 29 M.V.S. moved to the Reserve or Rest area at HEILLY.	
"	22/2/17 to 27/2/17		Inspection duty.	
"	28/2/17		Attended conference of AD's V.S. at office of the DDVS. Fourth Army. Inspection duty.	
			During the month very few cases were evacuated to L of C. firstly owing to the fact that no evacuations are allowed from units affected with Contagious Stomatitis and secondly the Railway was closed for a fortnight. Owing to these facts mange had to be treated in the unit lines and thorough segregation was impossible, as owing to the exceptionally severe frost everything was frozen and only one water point was available at which thousands of animals had to be watered daily.	
			W R Neale Major ADVS. 17th Division	

A5834 Wt. W4973/M687 750,000 8/16 D. D. & L. Ltd. Forms/C.2118/13.

Sheet No 1

Instructions regarding War Diaries and Intelligence Summaries are contained in F. S. Regs., Part II. and the Staff Manual respectively. Title pages will be prepared in manuscript.

WAR DIARY
~~or~~
~~INTELLIGENCE~~ SUMMARY.

(*Erase heading not required.*)

Army Form C. 2118.

of Major W. W. R. Neale AVC
ADVS. 17th Division

Vol 21

Place	Date	Hour	Summary of Events and Information	Remarks and references to Appendices
HEILLY	1/3/17		Inspecting Contagious Stomatitis and Mange Cases in the Divisional Artillery units at CARNOY.	
"	2/3/17		The Division moved from HEILLY to CONTAY leaving the 4th Army and joining the 5th Army. Inspecting units of the 50th Infantry Bde Group.	
CONTAY	3/3/17		DDVS. Fifth Army came to see me and inspect 29 M.V.S. at HARPONVILLE	
"	4/3/17		Inspected the Artillery units previous to their move tomorrow from the 4th to the 5th Army. Sent all Stomatitis Contagiosa cases to the 6th Reserve Park as per instructions from DDVS. Fourth Army.	
"	5/3/17 to 7/3/17		Inspecting units of Infantry Brigade Groups	
"	8/3/17		Proceeded to ALBERT and inspected the 78th Bde RFA	
"	9/3/17		Attended a conference of ADsVS. at Office of DDVS. Fifth Army.	
"	10/3/17 to 13/3/17		Inspection duty.	V.S. 4232 1-4-17

A5834 Wt. W4973/M687 750,000 8/16 D. D. & L. Ltd. Forms/C.2118/13.

Sheet No 2

Instructions regarding War Diaries and Intelligence Summaries are contained in F. S. Regs., Part II. and the Staff Manual respectively. Title pages will be prepared in manuscript.

WAR DIARY

~~or~~

~~INTELLIGENCE~~ SUMMARY.

(Erase heading not required.)

Army Form C. 2118.

of Major W. R. Neale AVC
ADVS. 17th Division

Place	Date	Hour	Summary of Events and Information	Remarks and references to Appendices
CONTAY	14/3/17		29 M.V.S marched via BEAUVAL and BOUVEMAISON for WILLEMAN. Infantry Brigades marching for new area.	
"	15/3/17		Moved from CONTAY to WILLEMAN leaving the 5th and joining the 3rd Army.	
"	16/3/17		29 M.V.S. marched into WILLEMAN and billeted there. Routine work.	
WILLEMAN	17/3/17 to 22/3/17		Inspection duty.	
"	23/3/17		Headquarters and 29 M.V.S. moved from WILLEMAN to LE CAUROY.	
"	24/3/17 to 26/3/17		Inspection duty.	
"	27/3/17		Routine work.	
"	28/3/17 to 31/3/17	}	On leave to U.K.	

A. D. V. S.
No. 48.1232
Date 1-4-17
17th DIVISION

W R Neale Major
ADVS. 17th Division

A5834 Wt. W4973/M687 750,000 8/16 D. D. & L. Ltd. Forms/C.2118/13.

Sheet No 1 –

Instructions regarding War Diaries and Intelligence Summaries are contained in F. S. Regs., Part II. and the Staff Manual respectively. Title pages will be prepared in manuscript.

WAR DIARY
or
~~INTELLIGENCE SUMMARY.~~
(Erase heading not required.)

of Major W W R Meale AVC
ADVS 17th Division

Army Form C. 2118.

Vol 22

Place	Date	Hour	Summary of Events and Information	Remarks and references to Appendices
	1.4.17 to 9.4.17		On leave of absence to U.K. and journey to rejoin the Division –	
In the Field			The greater part of the month was very cold with a lot of snow and rain. This, together with the animal ration being reduced to 3/4 the full ration affected the condition of the horses particularly the H.D.	
			From 11/4/17 to 25/4/17 the 17th Divisional Artillery were under my Administration and the opportunity was taken to evacuate all badly debilitated horses and those suffering from mange –	
			Mange during this month decidedly on the decrease –	
			No cases of Contagious Stomatitis occurred in the animals of the Division	
			A few cases of Ulcerative Cellulitis occurred but these were evacuated and means taken to prevent spread.	
			Cases of Necrotic Dermatitis and Picked up nail much fewer this month than during previous month	

A5834 Wt. W4973/M687 750,000 8/16 D. D. & L. Ltd. Forms/C.2118/13.

Sheet No 2

Army Form C. 2118.

Instructions regarding War Diaries and Intelligence Summaries are contained in F. S. Regs., Part II. and the Staff Manual respectively. Title pages will be prepared in manuscript.

WAR DIARY
or
~~INTELLIGENCE SUMMARY.~~

(*Erase heading not required.*)

of Major W. W. Neale A.V.C. A.D.V.S. 17th Division

Place	Date	Hour	Summary of Events and Information	Remarks and references to Appendices
In the Field	April 1917		The last week of the month was fine and dry and the full forage ration was issued - The condition of the animals greatly improved during the latter part of the month - On 25/4/17 the Divisional Artillery ceased to be under my administration - Losses from Shell fire during the month were heavy - W. W. Neale Major A.V.C. A.D.V.S. 17th Division	

A5834 Wt. W4973/M687 750,000 8/16 D. D. & L. Ltd. Forms/C.2118/13.

Instructions regarding War Diaries and Intelligence Summaries are contained in F. S. Regs., Part II. and the Staff Manual respectively. Title pages will be prepared in manuscript.

WAR DIARY ~~or~~ ~~INTELLIGENCE SUMMARY~~ of Major W. W. R. Neale AVC ADVS. 17th Division

(Erase heading not required.)

Army Form C. 2118.

Vol 23

Place	Date	Hour	Summary of Events and Information	Remarks and references to Appendices
In the Field	1/5/17 to 31/5/17		During this month the animals improved enormously in condition particularly the Artillery and Divisional Train horses. The weather was fine, dry and warm - draught work easy and the distances for delivering ammunition not very great. The forage ration was consistently good throughout the month and some grazing was obtainable during the latter portion. The remainder of the Debilitated and Mange Cases were evacuated to the L of C. A few cases of Ulcerative Cellulitis still crop up and also several cases of Tetanus occurred. It is hoped by injecting Anti Tetanic serum into all cases of deep shell wounds + wounds of the foot to prevent the latter disease. W. R. Neale Major ADVS 17th Division	

V.S. 4624
4-6-17.

A5834 Wt. W4973/M687 750,000 8/16 D. D. & L. Ltd. Forms/C.2118/13.

Instructions regarding War Diaries and Intelligence Summaries are contained in F. S. Regs., Part II. and the Staff Manual respectively. Title pages will be prepared in manuscript.

WAR DIARY
~~or~~
~~INTELLIGENCE SUMMARY~~.
(Erase heading not required.)

of Major W R Neale AVC
DADVS. 17th Division

Army Form C. 2118.

Vol 24

Place	Date	Hour	Summary of Events and Information	Remarks and references to Appendices
In the Field	1/6/17 to 30/6/17		During the month the condition of the animals continued to improve. The ration was consistently good throughout the month and plenty of green food was procured and fed to the horses & mules. The weather was fine throughout the month and at the beginning ~~[illegible]~~ abnormally hot. The Artillery during the first three weeks were not under the administration of the Division and at my first inspection when they did come under the Division I found that mange had made its re-appearance and had spread to a large number of animals. The affected animals were at once evacuated and strong measures taken to prevent further spread of the disease. Only a few cases of Ulcerative Cellulitis occurred during this month. Only two cases of Tetanus occurred in the Division during the month. W R Neale Major DADVS 17th Division	

A5834 Wt. W4973/M687 750,000 8/16 D. D. & L. Ltd. Forms/C.2118/13.

Sheet 1

Instructions regarding War Diaries and Intelligence Summaries are contained in F. S. Regs., Part II. and the Staff Manual respectively. Title pages will be prepared in manuscript.

WAR DIARY
or
~~INTELLIGENCE SUMMARY~~.
(Erase heading not required.)

of Major W. W. R. Meale A.V.C. D.A.D.V.S. 17th Division

Army Form C. 2118.

Vol 25

Place	Date	Hour	Summary of Events and Information	Remarks and references to Appendices
In the Field	1/7/17 to 31/7/17		During the month the chief work was combating Mange. This disease had made considerable headway but by at once evacuating undoubted cases and isolating anything the least suspicious, washing these with solution of Calcium Sulphide, disinfecting head collars daily, all line gear, and grooming kit regularly as a matter of stable routine the disease was nearly eradicated. Cases of so called Ophthalmia very much on the increase. A Bacteriologist from No 19 C.C.S. kindly gave me his assistance in endeavouring to find out the cause of this disease and he is still working on it. Isolated cases of Ulcerative Cellulitis still occur and it is noticed that cured cases coming up as Remounts frequently break out afresh and have to be evacuated. Only one case of Tetanus occurred in the Division during the month. The weather was good and the forage ration consistently good.	

Sheet No 2.

Instructions regarding War Diaries and Intelligence Summaries are contained in F. S. Regs., Part II. and the Staff Manual respectively. Title pages will be prepared in manuscript.

WAR DIARY

~~or~~

~~INTELLIGENCE SUMMARY.~~

(*Erase heading not required.*)

of Major W R Meale AVC DADVS 17th Division

Army Form C. 2118.

Place	Date	Hour	Summary of Events and Information	Remarks and references to Appendices
In the Field	1/7/17 to 31/7/17		On the 27th ult. the Division was reduced by one Veterinary Officer Captain A. Jackson A.V.C (T.C) being transferred to the 4th Division —	
			W R Meale Major DADVS 17th Division	

A5834 Wt. W4973/M687 750,000 8/16 D. D. & L. Ltd. Forms/C.2118/13.

Army Form C. 2118.

Instructions regarding War Diaries and Intelligence Summaries are contained in F. S. Regs., Part II. and the Staff Manual respectively. Title pages will be prepared in manuscript.

WAR DIARY
or
~~INTELLIGENCE SUMMARY.~~
(Erase heading not required.)

August

D.A.D.V.S.
17 Division
Vol 26

Place	Date	Hour	Summary of Events and Information	Remarks and references to Appendices
St NICHOLAS	1.		Inspected mange cases at 79 Bde R.F.A and 78 Bde R.F.A and found suspected cases getting cured.	
"	2		Conference with the V.O's of the division.	
"	3		Visited Mob. Vet. Sec. + inspected 78 and 93. Field Co. R.E.	
"			Malleined all the animals of 236 Machine Gun Co. on their arrival to the division	
"	4		Attended conference at [illegible] Corps H.Q. of the A.D.V.S.	
"	5		Inspected 1 + 2 Sections. 17 D.A.C.	
"	6		Visited Mob. Vet. Sec. + inspected the divisional train	
"	7.		Inspected The Royal West Surrey Regt.	
"	8		Inspected 78 Bde. R.F.A.	

A5834 Wt. W4973/M687 750,000 8/16 D. D. & L. Ltd. Forms/C.2118/13.

Instructions regarding War Diaries and Intelligence Summaries are contained in F. S. Regs., Part II. and the Staff Manual respectively. Title pages will be prepared in manuscript.

WAR DIARY
or
~~INTELLIGENCE SUMMARY.~~
(Erase heading not required.)

Army Form C. 2118.

August

D.A.D.V.S. 17 Division

Place	Date	Hour	Summary of Events and Information	Remarks and references to Appendices
St. Nicholas	9		Inspected 79 Bde. R.F.A	
"	10		Inspected 50 Bde. Transport Empt.	
"	11		Inspected 51 Bde Transport Unit.	
"	12		Inspected the horses at 79 Bde R.F.A. prior to their admittance to XVII Corps horse rest Camp.	
"	13		Visited Mob Vet. Sec and 79 Bde R.F.A. Sick lines.	
"	14		at Corps HQ while ADVS is on Sick list. Visited Mob. Vet. Sec.	
"	15		Visited Corps H.Q. Mob. Vet. Sec. Inspected Sickness animals of the different units of the division	
"	16		Inspected 17 Div Train. 17 Signal Co. and Corps H.Q.	
"	17		Office Routine	

A5834 Wt. W4973/M687 750,000 8/16 D. D. & L. Ltd. Forms/C.2118/13.

Instructions regarding War Diaries and Intelligence Summaries are contained in F. S. Regs., Part II. and the Staff Manual respectively. Title pages will be prepared in manuscript.

WAR DIARY
or
INTELLIGENCE SUMMARY.
(*Erase heading not required.*)

August

Army Form C. 2118.

D.A.D.V.S.
17 Division

Place	Date	Hour	Summary of Events and Information	Remarks and references to Appendices
St NICHOLAS.	18		Inspected all Field Ambulance Transport	
	19.		Office Routine at XVII Corps HQ.	
	20		Inspected Batteries of 78 Bde R.F.A	
	21		Office Routine at Corps and division	
	22		Inspected 79 Bde R.F.A	
	23.- 31.		Proceeded to England on leave of absence, Capt. H. S. Lowel. O.C 29 Mob Vet Sec to carry on as D.A.D.V.S	
	24.		Inspected all the animals of the Train and found the animals in excellent condition, the animals of No. 1 and No. 2 Co's standing out for excellence.	

A5834 Wt. W4973/M687 750,000 8/16 D. D. & L. Ltd. Forms/C.2118/13.

Army Form C. 2118.

WAR DIARY
or
~~INTELLIGENCE SUMMARY.~~

(Erase heading not required.)

Instructions regarding War Diaries and Intelligence Summaries are contained in F. S. Regs., Part II. and the Staff Manual respectively. Title pages will be prepared in manuscript.

August

Place	Date	Hour	Summary of Events and Information	Remarks and references to Appendices
St NICHOLAS.	25		Inspected 17 Signal Co and found the transport in good order - This unit is good in horse mastership the animals being always well turned out. Some of the animals were on the thin side due to the heavy night work that they had been doing of late. Inspecting mares suitable for breeding purposes and selected three animals from Div H.Q for Corps Committee to see. Inspected all the mares suitable for breeding and selected 50 animals for the Corps Committee to see.	
	26		Visited the Battery lines of 78 Bde R.F.A to see their	

A5834 Wt. W4973/M687 750,000 8/16 D. D. & L. Ltd. Forms/C.2118/13.

Instructions regarding War Diaries and Intelligence Summaries are contained in F. S. Regs., Part II. and the Staff Manual respectively. Title pages will be prepared in manuscript.

December

WAR DIARY
or
INTELLIGENCE SUMMARY.
(Erase heading not required.)

ADVS
17 Division

Army Form C. 2118.

Place	Date	Hour	Summary of Events and Information	Remarks and references to Appendices
			proposed winter standings and found that the lines will be too far away from main Road, if roads to the horse lines are made it will entail a great deal of labour. Suggestions were put to CRA that lines be brought nearer the Road.	
	27		Visited horse lines of 77 Bde R.F.A. to see their winter standings and the position with the exception of one Battery was good. Suggested that one site be selected for this battery.	
	28		Inspected the Div Amm Col horses and their proposed	

Instructions regarding War Diaries and Intelligence Summaries are contained in F. S. Regs., Part II. and the Staff Manual respectively. Title pages will be prepared in manuscript.

WAR DIARY
or
INTELLIGENCE SUMMARY.
(*Erase heading not required.*)

August

DADVS 17 Divn

Army. Form C. 2118.

Place	Date	Hour	Summary of Events and Information	Remarks and references to Appendices
St NICHOLAS	28		Win to Standings: The attention to detail that this unit pays to the animals is marked and all their animals show excellent condition. The horse mastership of this large unit is very good & the site for the winter standings excellent.	
	29.		Office Routine at Divisional H.Q.	
"	30		Attended with Brood mares for Corps Committee to see - 13 animals suitable for Brood mares for artillery work were selected & animals were branded. The condition and good looks of these mares reflected with credit on the division as the standard aimed at by the Judges was very high and the test a severe one.	
	31.		Office work at H.Q.	

J J R. Kennedy Capt
a/ADVS
17 Divn

A5834 Wt. W4973/M687 750,000 8/16 D. D. & L. Ltd. Forms/C.2118/13.

Sheet No 1.

Instructions regarding War Diaries and Intelligence Summaries are contained in F. S. Regs., Part II. and the Staff Manual respectively. Title pages will be prepared in manuscript.

WAR DIARY

~~or~~

~~INTELLIGENCE SUMMARY.~~

(Erase heading not required.)

of Major W. W. R. Neale AVC. Army Form C. 2118.

DADVS. 17th Division

Vol 27

Place	Date	Hour	Summary of Events and Information	Remarks and references to Appendices
In the Field	Septr 1st to 24th		During this period the Division was in the forward area. The health of the animals has been consistently good and their condition has been maintained. Only a few isolated cases of Mange occurred and these were evacuated as soon as the disease was definitely diagnosed. A certain number of cases of Ulcerative Cellulitis continue to crop up which are immediately transferred to the Mobile Veterinary Section for evacuation to the Base. During the month Tetanus has been on the increase and further instructions were issued to Veterinary Officers to use Anti Tetanic in the case of all serious wounds. Stabling and standings for the winter were commenced, well pushed forward and in some cases finished by all units of the Division. The weather during the month was very good consequently the going on roads and cross country tracks used by animals was easy.	

Sheet No 2.

Instructions regarding War Diaries and Intelligence Summaries are contained in F. S. Regs., Part II. and the Staff Manual respectively. Title pages will be prepared in manuscript.

WAR DIARY

~~or~~

~~INTELLIGENCE SUMMARY.~~

(Erase heading not required.)

of Major W. W. R. Neale AVC.
DADVS. 17th Division

Army Form C. 2118.

Place	Date	Hour	Summary of Events and Information	Remarks and references to Appendices
In the Field	Sept. 25th to 30th		During this period the Division less Artillery was in the back area. The conditions were good except that in most places water was scarce and animals had to go a long way for it.	
			W. R. Neale Major DADVS. 17th Division	

A5834 Wt. W4973/M687 750,000 8/16 D. D. & L. Ltd. Forms/C.2118/13.

Instructions regarding War Diaries and Intelligence Summaries are contained in F. S. Regs., Part II. and the Staff Manual respectively. Title pages will be prepared in manuscript.

WAR DIARY ~~or~~ ~~INTELLIGENCE SUMMARY.~~

(*Erase heading not required.*)

of Major W. G. R. Neale DADVS. 17th Division

Army Form C. 2118.

Vol 28

Place	Date	Hour	Summary of Events and Information	Remarks and references to Appendices
In the Field	Octr 1917.		During this period the animals had no standings or stables and owing to there being a lot of rain, the standings became very bad and Necrosis made its appearance. Casualties from shell fire were rather severe, most of the cases occurring whilst taking up ammunition by pack. A few casualties were caused by bomb dropped by enemy aircraft. There were extremely few cases of Mange during the month, very little Tetanus but about the usual number of cases of Ulcerative Cellulitis. The condition of the animals remained satisfactory. W.G.R. Neale Major DADVS. 17th Division	

A5834 Wt. W4973/M687 750,000 8/16 D. D. & L. Ltd. Forms/C.2118/13.

Sheet No 1

Instructions regarding War Diaries and Intelligence Summaries are contained in F. S. Regs., Part II. and the Staff Manual respectively. Title pages will be prepared in manuscript.

WAR DIARY
or
~~INTELLIGENCE SUMMARY.~~
(*Erase heading not required.*)

of Major W. W. R. Steale A.V.C. DADVS. 17th Division

Army Form C. 2118.

Vol 29

Place	Date	Hour	Summary of Events and Information	Remarks and references to Appendices
In the Field	Nov. 1st to Nov. 30th 1917		The first week of the month the Division was in the rest area and the animals had no standings or shelters. The ground was wet and the horse lines very bad. Necrotic ulcers of the heels, pasterns &c began to make their appearance owing to these conditions. The last three weeks of the month were spent in the forward area; at first there were no stables but these were quickly built, and so cases of Necrotic dermatitis were rare. A few cases of Mange made their appearance during the month; these were immediately evacuated and precautions taken to prevent the disease spreading. Specific Ophthalmia and Ulcerative Cellulitis are both on the increase. The former disease does well when ~~immediately~~ treated with an injection of Lugols solution of Iodine as soon as discovered. The 17th Divisional Artillery were not under my administration during	

A5834 Wt. W4973/M687 750,000 8/16 D. D. & L. Ltd. Forms/C.2118/13.

Sheet 2.

Instructions regarding War Diaries and Intelligence Summaries are contained in F. S. Regs., Part II. and the Staff Manual respectively. Title pages will be prepared in manuscript.

WAR DIARY or ~~INTELLIGENCE SUMMARY~~. of Major W. W. R. Neale AVC DADVS 17th Division

(*Erase heading not required.*)

Army Form C. 2118.

Place	Date	Hour	Summary of Events and Information	Remarks and references to Appendices
In the field	Nov. 1917		my part of the month so I have been unable to inspect it. The weather on the whole was poor. The animals kept their condition very well, work was not severe and forage on the whole was good.	
			W R Neale Major DADVS 17th Division	

A5834 Wt. W4973/M687 750,000 8/16 D. D. & L. Ltd. Forms/C.2118/13.

Sheet No 14

Instructions regarding War Diaries and Intelligence Summaries are contained in F. S. Regs., Part II. and the Staff Manual respectively. Title pages will be prepared in manuscript.

WAR DIARY
or
INTELLIGENCE SUMMARY.
(*Erase heading not required.*)

of Major W. W. R. Steale AVC. DADVS. 17th Division

Army Form C. 2118.

Vol 30

Place	Date	Hour	Summary of Events and Information	Remarks and references to Appendices
In the Field	Decr 1st to 31st 1917		During the first half of the month in Belgium the great majority of the animals were in stables and there was very little disease. Most of the casualties were caused by Bomb and Shell fire. Cases of Specific Ophthalmia still continued to occur but were immediately treated with an injection of Lugols solution and most made a good recovery. Only a few cases of mange occurred during the month and these were evacuated as soon as diagnosed. Ulcerative Cellulitis decreased during this period. The last half of the month was frosty with some snow. The ground was slippery and frozen hard and at first, owing to inadequate winter shoeing animals were continually falling and were unable to get a foothold. The area occupied by the animals on this front (CAMBRAI) was infected with STOMATITIS CONTAGIOSA and one case occurred in	

A5834 Wt. W4973/M687 750,000 8/16 D. D. & L. Ltd. Forms/C.2118/13.

Sheet No 2

Instructions regarding War Diaries and Intelligence Summaries are contained in F. S. Regs., Part II. and the Staff Manual respectively. Title pages will be prepared in manuscript.

WAR DIARY
or
INTELLIGENCE SUMMARY.

(Erase heading not required.)

of Major W. W. R. Neale AVC DADVS 17th Division

Army Form C. 2118.

Place	Date	Hour	Summary of Events and Information	Remarks and references to Appendices
In the Field	Decr 1st to 31st 1917		in the Division (10th Lancashire Fusiliers) on the last day of the month. This unit had its transport lines in BERTINCOURT where the disease had already made its appearance among the 47th Div. Artillery. The 17th Divisional Artillery were away from the Division the whole of the month.	

W. W. R. Neale Major
DADVS 17th Division

A5834 Wt. W4973/M687 750,000 8/16 D. D. & L. Ltd. Forms/C.2118/13.

Sheet No 1

Army Form C. 2118.

WAR DIARY
or
INTELLIGENCE SUMMARY.
(Erase heading not required.)

of Major W. W. R. Neale AVC
DADVS. 17th Division

Vol 31

Instructions regarding War Diaries and Intelligence Summaries are contained in F. S. Regs., Part II. and the Staff Manual respectively. Title pages will be prepared in manuscript.

Place	Date	Hour	Summary of Events and Information	Remarks and references to Appendices
In the Field YTRES.	Jan 1918		No further cases of STOMATITIS CONTAGIOSA occurred, that is to say only one case in the Division so far this year. To prevent the spread of this disease the affected animal was immediately transferred to the 1/2 London M.V.S. which was used as a Stomatitis Hospital and water troughs disinfected with Chloride of Lime. During the first few days of the month the roads were very slippery owing to frost and frozen snow. The frost cogs were not very satisfactory, those in partly worn shoes not having sufficient hold of the shoe and quickly coming out and when the shoes were practically new many of the cogs were found to be made of very brittle metal and snapped off in some part of the screw thread. The Artillery rejoined the Division this month. With the exception of a few sporadic cases of mange and a few debility cases there is very little sickness amongst the Artillery animals and their condition on the whole is very good. In two units viz the 52nd Machine Gun Company and the 17th Signal Company	

A5834 Wt. W4973/M687 750,000 8/16 D. D. & L. Ltd. Forms/C.2118/13.

Sheet No 2

Instructions regarding War Diaries and Intelligence Summaries are contained in F. S. Regs., Part II. and the Staff Manual respectively. Title pages will be prepared in manuscript.

WAR DIARY
~~or~~
INTELLIGENCE SUMMARY.
(*Erase heading not required.*)

of Major W. W. R. Neale AVC
DADVS. 17th Division

Army Form C. 2118.

Place	Date	Hour	Summary of Events and Information	Remarks and references to Appendices
In the Field YTRES	Jany 1918		Slight cases of head & neck mange occurred, the worst cases were evacuated but the milder cases were isolated, clipped and dressed with Calcium Sulphide solution.	
			Towards the end of the month the corn ration was cut down by 2 lbs per animal per day.	
			Standings were made for ~~[illegible]~~ the 78th and 79th Brigades R.F.A. and standings built for the Infantry Brigade Groups. The 17th D.A.C. went into the back area on the 8th inst: and were not with the Division.	
			W R Neale Major DADVS 17th Division	

A5834 Wt. W4973/M687 750,000 8/16 D. D. & L. Ltd. Forms/C.2118/13.

13

Instructions regarding War Diaries and Intelligence Summaries are contained in F. S. Regs., Part II. and the Staff Manual respectively. Title pages will be prepared in manuscript.

Army Form C. 2118.

WAR DIARY
~~or~~
~~INTELLIGENCE SUMMARY.~~
(Erase heading not required.)

of Major W. W. R. Neale AVC
DADVS. 17th Division

VR 32

Place	Date	Hour	Summary of Events and Information	Remarks and references to Appendices
In the Field YTRES & BERTINCOURT	Feby 1st to 28th 1918		This was a very good month for animals, being fine and mild and all the animals having good standings. Owing to these conditions and no very hard work the reduction of 2 lbs per head per day of the Oat ration has not adversely affected the condition of the animals. A few Sporadic cases of Mange continue to make their appearance but there is no big outbreak of the disease. A large number of animals are affected with lice. Dipping in the Corps Horse Dip is going to be carried out when the bath is available but until the animals lose their heavy winter coats it will be difficult to eradicate the lice. The number of cases of Specific Ophthalmia is still serious but the treatment with Lugols solution is fairly successful. Very few cases of Ulcerative Cellulitis are now occurring in the Division. Three cases of Tetanus have occurred but are still under treatment and progressing favourably. W R Neale Major AVC DADVS. 17th Division	

A5834 Wt. W4973/M687 750,000 8/16 D. D. & L. Ltd. Forms/C.2118/13.

Sheet No 1 17

Instructions regarding War Diaries and Intelligence Summaries are contained in F. S. Regs., Part II. and the Staff Manual respectively. Title pages will be prepared in manuscript.

WAR DIARY

or

INTELLIGENCE SUMMARY.

(Erase heading not required.)

of Major W. W. R. Neale AVC. DADVS. 17th Division

Army Form C. 2118.

Vol 33

Place	Date	Hour	Summary of Events and Information	Remarks and references to Appendices
In the Field BERTINCOURT	March 1st to 20th 1918.		Very few casualties amongst animals during this period. The first five days were cold with some snow and rain but after this the weather became very fine and warm. The three cases of Tetanus mentioned in the Diary for February all recovered. Nearly all animals of the Division were passed through the Vth Corps Horse Dip.	
"	March 21st		German attack began at 5 am. VELU WOOD in which were situated the wagon lines of the 78th and 79th Brigade R.F.A and some of the Infantry Transport was heavily shelled and many animals were killed. The wood was evacuated as quickly as possible but it was not possible to get away many stores. Captain Hill AVC (T.C) who was in Veterinary charge of the two Artillery Brigades lost his Veterinary chest and wallet and some of the attached AVC Sergeants lost their Veterinary wallets. Rear Head Quarters retired to TIEAULENCOURT	
In the Field	March 22nd		Rear Echelon retired to DESTREMONT FARM. LE SARS.	
	March 23rd		Went to Army HQ in ALBERT to attend conference of DVS but on arrival there found conference had been postponed but the notification had not reached me.	

A5834 Wt. W4973/M687 750,000 8/16 D. D. & L. Ltd. Forms/C.2118/13.

Sheet No. 2

Instructions regarding War Diaries and Intelligence Summaries are contained in F. S. Regs., Part II. and the Staff Manual respectively. Title pages will be prepared in manuscript.

WAR DIARY
or
INTELLIGENCE SUMMARY.

(Erase heading not required.)

of Major W. W. R Neale AVC
DADVS 17th Division

Army Form C. 2118.

Place	Date	Hour	Summary of Events and Information	Remarks and references to Appendices
In the Field	March 24th		Rear Echelon H.Q. retired first to LA BOISELLE and later to HENNENCOURT.	
"	March 25th		Was able to visit several units in the morning. Water for animals in this retirement is a difficulty, the only available water being village ponds which are very foul. Many animals refuse water altogether and none drink properly. Rear Echelon and all Infantry Transport retired to VADENCOURT and CONTAY also the DAC.	
"	March 26th		Visited all unit transport lines to ascertain number of animal casualties for the information of Q. branch. Rear Echelon moved first to SENLIS in the evening and later marched all night to PUCHEVILLERS via FORCEVILLE. ACHEUX - LEALVILLERS and TOUTENCOURT.	
"	March 27+28		Remained in PUCHEVILLERS - Visiting units.	
"	March 29		Rear Echelon H.Q. moved from PUCHEVILLERS to MIRVAUX.	
"	March 30+31		Remained in MIRVAUX. Was able to go round all Batteries of the 78th and 79th Brigades RFA at SENLIS and HARPONVILLE for the first time since the attack commenced.	

W R Neale Major AVC
D.A.D.V.S. 17th Division

A5834 Wt. W4973/M687 750,000 8/16 D. D. & L. Ltd. Forms/C.2118/13.

24

Instructions regarding War Diaries and Intelligence Summaries are contained in F. S. Regs., Part II. and the Staff Manual respectively. Title pages will be prepared in manuscript.

WAR DIARY
or
~~INTELLIGENCE SUMMARY.~~
(Erase heading not required.)

of Major W. W. R. Neale AVC.
DADVS. 17th Division

Army Form C. 2118.

Vol 34

Place	Date	Hour	Summary of Events and Information	Remarks and references to Appendices
In the Field [illegible]	1/4/18 30/4/18		During this month there was very little disease amongst the animals of the Division – Mange was entirely eradicated. Cases of Lice which were numerous and severe are now that the animals are losing their winter coats being satisfactorily dealt with. A good many animals lost condition during the month, particularly those which had come up clipped from the Base. Another cause of loss of condition was bad and insufficient water at many places where the animals were picketed. Cases of Specific Ophthalmia continue to occur most of them being recurrent cases and a large number of these eventually go blind. Only very few cases of Ulcerative Cellulitis are now being met with in the Division – One case of Tetanus occurred in a mule which is still remaining under treatment and progressing favourably. On the whole the weather conditions were good for the time of year, although there was frequently very cold winds which caused loss of condition. No 2454 P/A/Sergt COTTRELL A.V.C. attached 51st Infantry Brigade was wounded by shell fire on April 23rd and evacuated. No 2858 S/A/Sergt WOOD C. AVC. attached No 1 Section 17th DAC. was evacuated sick on 19/4/18 Large casualties were caused by shell fire during the month. W. W. R. Neale Major DADVS 17th Division	

A5834 Wt. W4973/M687 750,000 8/16 D. D. & L. Ltd. Forms/C.2118/13.

19 Army Form C. 2118. 17

Instructions regarding War Diaries and Intelligence Summaries are contained in F. S. Regs., Part II. and the Staff Manual respectively. Title pages will be prepared in manuscript.

WAR DIARY or ~~INTELLIGENCE SUMMARY~~.

(*Erase heading not required.*)

of Major W. W. R. Meale A.V.C.
D.A.D.V.S. 17th Division

Vol 35

Place	Date	Hour	Summary of Events and Information	Remarks and references to Appendices
In the Field	1/5/18 to 31/5/18		This was a good month for animals, being for the most part fine and the ground dry & hard. A few sporadic cases of Mange made their appearance chiefly in the Artillery and these were evacuated as soon as discovered. The case of Tetanus which was under treatment at the beginning of the month made a good recovery. Many cases of Specific Ophthalmia occurred during the month, this disease being a very serious one, although recovery usually takes place from the first attack, in nearly every case the disease recurs & in many cases blindness ensues. A few cases of Ulcerative Cellulitis continue to make their appearance chiefly amongst draught horses. During the month the animals have commenced to pick up condition which was lost in ~~the~~ the latter part of March & during April. Captain Kippel A.V.C. (S.R.) O.C. 29 M.V.S. was absent from the Division sick from May 15th to May 30th 1918.	
			W. R. Meale Major D.A.D.V.S. 17th Division	

A5834 Wt. W4973/M687 750,000 8/16 D. D. & L. Ltd. Forms/C.2118/13.

Instructions regarding War Diaries and Intelligence Summaries are contained in F. S. Regs., Part II. and the Staff Manual respectively. Title pages will be prepared in manuscript.

17.

WAR DIARY of Major W.W.R. Neale AVC DADVS. 17th Division
or
~~INTELLIGENCE SUMMARY.~~

(Erase heading not required.)

Army Form C. 2118.

Vol 36

Place	Date	Hour	Summary of Events and Information	Remarks and references to Appendices
In the Field	1/6/18 to 30/6/18		This was a very fine month and consequently good for animals – Only a few showers fell during the whole of the month. On June 12th the DDVS 3rd Army accompanied by the D.D.V. inspected the Divisional Artillery. Green forage was obtainable during the whole month and the forage ration was on the whole good although occasionally too much straw in lieu of hay was issued – Occasionally Maize and Barley in small quantities were issued in lieu of Oats – Animals improved in condition during the month – Ophthalmia was the most serious disease encountered and many animals went blind & had to be evacuated. A few cases of Mange and Ulcerative Cellulitis continue to occur but not to any extent and when discovered they are immediately evacuated. Captain Hull AVC att'd to the Divisional Artillery met with an accident to his [illegible] on June 11th which led to his being [illegible] to the [illegible] on June 23rd. W.R. Neale Major DADVS. 17th Division	

19

Instructions regarding War Diaries and Intelligence Summaries are contained in F. S. Regs., Part II. and the Staff Manual respectively. Title pages will be prepared in manuscript.

WAR DIARY ~~or INTELLIGENCE SUMMARY.~~ of Major W.W.R. Neale A.V.C. D.A.D.V.S. 17th Division

(Erase heading not required.)

Army Form C. 2118.

VOL 37

Place	Date	Hour	Summary of Events and Information	Remarks and references to Appendices
In the Field	1/7/18 to 31/7/18		Specific Ophthalmia and Amaurosis, blindness &c resulting from recurrent attacks of this disease continues to be a very serious cause of wastage among animals of the Division. Three slight cases of head mange were discovered in the Divisional Artillery during the month and evacuated. One case of Ulcerative Cellulitis occurred and was at once evacuated. The hay ration was cut down to 9 lbs per animal per day and this probably caused some animals to lose condition, although most units were able to supplement their forage ration by getting clover &c from the forward area. Three Batteries of the 79th Brigade R.F.A. lost a lot of condition during the month viz A, C and D. The horses of C Battery fell off to an alarming extent & I attribute this to want of supervision and to not having an officer permanently in the Wagon Lines. Officers down from the firing line for a few days want rest & do not appear to take very much interest in the well being of the horses. W R Neale Major D.A.D.V.S. 17th Division	

A5834 Wt. W4973/M687 750,000 8/16 D. D. & L. Ltd. Forms/C.2118/13.

Sheet 1. 24

Of Major W. W. R. Neale AVC
DADVS 17th Division

Army Form C. 2118.

Instructions regarding War Diaries and Intelligence Summaries are contained in F. S. Regs., Part II. and the Staff Manual respectively. Title pages will be prepared in manuscript.

WAR DIARY
or
INTELLIGENCE SUMMARY.
(Erase heading not required.)

VR 38

Place	Date	Hour	Summary of Events and Information	Remarks and references to Appendices
In the Field (TOUTENCOURT)	Aug 12th to Aug 7th 1918.		During this period the animals of the Division on the whole maintained their good condition with the exception of "C" and "D" Batteries 79th Brigade RFA whose horses are poor and the 10th Lancashire Fusiliers whose condition is not up to the standard of other Infantry units. The condition of C/79 RFA I attribute to lack of supervision and bad stable management. D/79 RFA a Howitzer Battery, has had a lot of hard work carrying ammunition & this together with the reduced ration is chiefly the cause of loss of condition in this Battery. The Lancashire Fus^s have had no Transport Officer for some time. On August 7th the DDVS Third Army accompanied by ADVS Vth Corps inspected the Divisional Artillery.	
ALLONVILLE & HAMELET	Aug 8th 17th		On August 8th the Division moved to ALLONVILLE leaving the Third Army and joined the Australian Corps, Fourth Army and on August 13th moved to Camp near HAMELET. During the ten days in this Corps the animals improved a good deal in condition as the work was light and plenty of food obtainable in forward areas to supplement the ordinary ration.	

A5834 Wt. W4973/M687 750,000 8/16 D. D. & L. Ltd. Forms/C.2118/13.

Sheet No. 2.

Instructions regarding War Diaries and Intelligence Summaries are contained in F. S. Regs., Part II. and the Staff Manual respectively. Title pages will be prepared in manuscript.

WAR DIARY

or

INTELLIGENCE SUMMARY.

(Erase heading not required.)

of Major W. W. R. Neale AVC
DADVS. 17th Division

Army Form C. 2118.

Place	Date	Hour	Summary of Events and Information	Remarks and references to Appendices
In the Field TOUTENCOURT	Aug. 18-20 1918		On the 18th the Division left the Fourth Army and rejoined the Third Army. On August 20th I was ordered to Vth Corps H.Q. to act as ADVS. Vth Corps owing to Lt. Col. Glasse AVC ADVS. Vth Corps having been admitted to Hospital. Handed over my duties as DADVS. 17th Division to Capt. J. T. G. Kirkhill AVC and joined Vth Corps as A/ADVS.	

W. R. Neale Major
DADVS. 17th Division

A5834 Wt. W4973/M687 750,000 8/16 D. D. & L. Ltd. Forms/C.2118/13.

October 1918

Instructions regarding War Diaries and Intelligence Summaries are contained in F. S. Regs., Part II. and the Staff Manual respectively. Title pages will be prepared in manuscript.

WAR DIARY or INTELLIGENCE SUMMARY.

(*Erase heading not required.*)

of Major W W R Neale AVC DDVS 17th Division

Army Form C. 2118.

Place	Date	Hour	Summary of Events and Information	Remarks and references to Appendices
			During this period the Division was advancing rapidly and it was only occasionally possible to inspect units. The animals kept their condition well as there was good feeding & extra forage could often be obtained –	
			W R Neale Major DDVS 17 Division	

D. D. & L., London, E.C.
(A10266) Wt W5300/P713 750,000 2/18 Sch. 52 Forms/C2118/16

October 1918

Instructions regarding War Diaries and Intelligence Summaries are contained in F. S. Regs., Part II. and the Staff Manual respectively. Title pages will be prepared in manuscript.

WAR DIARY or INTELLIGENCE SUMMARY.

(Erase heading not required.)

of Major W W R Meikle D.A.D.V.S. 17 Division

Army Form C. 2118.

Oct '18

Place	Date	Hour	Summary of Events and Information	Remarks and references to Appendices
LECHELLE	Oct 1st – 5 Oct 6th		Inspecting the 17th D.A.C. and units of Infantry Brigade groups. On the 5th Advanced H.Q. moved to HEUDECOURT and 29 M.V.S. to near EQUANCOURT.	
HEUDECOURT	7th		Moved from LECHELLE to join advanced H.Q. Met A.D.V.S. V Corps. Wet. Cold	
"	8-9		Routine work. On 9th Advanced H.Q. moved to GUILLEMIN FARM leaving rear H.Q. at HEUDECOURT	
GUILLEMIN FARM	10		Advanced H.Q. moved to MONTIGNY and Rear H.Q. to GUILLEMIN FARM on the WALINCOURT - ESNES road.	
MONTIGNY	11		Moved from GUILLEMIN FARM to MONTIGNY.	
"	12-16		Inspecting 17 Divisional Train. S.A.A. Section 17 D.A.C. Captn KEPPEL A.V.C. O.C. 29 M.V.S. proceeded on leave on 13th. On 16th handed over duties of D.A.D.V.S. to Capt. NICHOLSON A.V.C. temporarily whilst I act as A.D.V.S. V Corps in the place of Lt Col CONDER D.S.O. who ~~[illegible]~~ acts as D.D.V.S. 3rd Army during the absence of Col PALLIN on leave	

D. D. & L., London, E.C. (A10266) Wt W5300/P713 750,000 2/18 Sch. 52 Forms/C2118/16

24

Instructions regarding War Diaries and Intelligence Summaries are contained in F. S. Regs., Part II. and the Staff Manual respectively. Title Pages will be prepared in manuscript.

WAR DIARY
or
~~INTELLIGENCE SUMMARY~~

(Erase heading not required.)

Army Form C. 2118.

of Major W. R. Meale AVC
DADVS. 17th Division

VIII 39

Place	Date	Hour	Summary of Events and Information	Remarks and references to Appendices
In the Field	23/9/16		Resumed duties of DADVS 17th Division from A/ADVS. V Corps.	
"	24/9/16 } 27/9/16 }		Routine work	
"	28/9/16		Attended conference of DADVS's at V Corps H.Q. – Office work.	
"	29/9/16		Inspection duty.	
"	30/9/16		Captain J. F. Thurston AVC who had been posted to the Division for temporary duty during my absence at the Corps left the Division for temporary duty with the 33rd Division –	

W. R. Meale Major
DADVS. 17th Division

2449 Wt. W14957/M90 750,000 1/16 J.B.C. & A. Forms/C.2118/12.

8

Instructions regarding War Diaries and Intelligence Summaries are contained in F. S. Regs., Part II. and the Staff Manual respectively. Title pages will be prepared in manuscript.

WAR DIARY
or
INTELLIGENCE SUMMARY.
(*Erase heading not required.*)

Army Form C. 2118.

DADVS
17 Division
November 1918

Vol 42

Place	Date	Hour	Summary of Events and Information	Remarks and references to Appendices
INCHY	2-5		Capt J.I.G. KEPPEL of 19 Mobile Vety Section took over duties of DADVS from Capt L NICHOLSON. Work from 2-5 November was of routine nature.	
INCHY – POIX du NORD.	5.		Office of DADVS moved with the mobile vety section to POIX du NORD.	
POIX du NORD	5-7.		Routine duty & office work. Inspected the transport of 17 Signal Co and found the horses poor.	
POIX du NORD – LOCQUIGNOL	7.		Took office with mobile vety section to LOCQUIGNOL in the FOREST de MORMAL.	
LOCQUIGNOL	7-8		Stood to waiting orders to move forward.	
LOCQUIGNOL – TETE NOIR	8		Marched to TETE NOIR for one night and then proceeded to divisional HQ which had been	
AULNOYE	8-12		established at AULNOYE.	

A5834 Wt. W4973/M687 750,000 8/16 D. D. & L. Ltd. Forms/C.2118/13.

Instructions regarding War Diaries and Intelligence Summaries are contained in F. S. Regs., Part II. and the Staff Manual respectively. Title Pages will be prepared in manuscript.

WAR DIARY
or
INTELLIGENCE SUMMARY
(Erase heading not required.)

Army Form C. 2118

Place	Date	Hour	Summary of Events and Information	Remarks and references to Appendices
AULNOYE	8-12		[illegible]	
AULNOYE	12		[illegible]	
VENDEGIES			[illegible]	
VENDEGIES – INCHY	13		[illegible]	
INCHY	13-17		[illegible]	

1875 Wt. W593/826 1,000,000 4/15 J.B.C. & A. A.D.S.S./Forms/C. 2118.

Instructions regarding War Diaries and Intelligence Summaries are contained in F. S. Regs., Part II. and the Staff Manual respectively. Title pages will be prepared in manuscript.

WAR DIARY of Major W. W. R. Neale AVC DADVS 17th Division

~~or INTELLIGENCE SUMMARY.~~

(Erase heading not required.)

Army Form C. 2118.

Place	Date	Hour	Summary of Events and Information	Remarks and references to Appendices
INCHY.	17/11/18		Returned from leave to U.K. and took over the duties of D.A.D.V.S. from Captain J. J. G. Keppel AVC (S.R.) who had been officiating during my absence.	
"	18/11/18 to 30/11/18		Routine work inspecting units of the Division. During this period, owing to the Armistice, the Division was at rest. Most of the Infantry animals were in good stables which were plentiful, as the civilian population had no animals, all of these having been taken by the Germans. The Artillery animals were picketed in the open. Advantage was taken of this period to evacuate old and thin horses the great majority of which were in the Artillery.	
			There was practically no disease amongst the animals, casualties being few and chiefly confined to injuries.	
			On the 19th Capt. P. W. Walker proceeded on 14 days leave of absence to the U.K.	
			W. R. Neale Major DADVS 17th Division	

D. D. & L., London, E.C.
(A10266) Wt W5300/P713 750,000 2/18 Sch. 52 Forms/C2118/16

November 1918.

WAR DIARY

of Major W.W.R. Neale A.V.C. D.A.D.V.S. 17th Division

Army Form C. 2118.

Nov. 18

or

INTELLIGENCE SUMMARY.

(*Erase heading not required.*)

Instructions regarding War Diaries and Intelligence Summaries are contained in F. S. Regs., Part II. and the Staff Manual respectively. Title pages will be prepared in manuscript.

Place	Date	Hour	Summary of Events and Information	Remarks and references to Appendices
	1-16		On leave to U.K.	
INCHY	17		Took over from Capt. KEPPEL A.V.C. on returning from leave.	
— " —	18-30		Inspection duty of all units of the Division and 155 A.F.A. Brigade which is under the administration of the 7th Division. On the 19th Capt WALKER A.V.C. proceeded on leave to U.K. for 14 days. During this period the animals improved in condition especially those of Infantry Brigade Groups as nearly all were in good stables and extra forage could often be obtained.	

W.R. Neale Major
D.A.D.V.S. 17th Division

D. D. & L., London, E.C.
(A10266) Wt W5300/P713 750,000 2/18 Sch. 52 Forms/C2118/16

December 1918

Instructions regarding War Diaries and Intelligence Summaries are contained in F. S. Regs., Part II. and the Staff Manual respectively. Title pages will be prepared in manuscript.

WAR DIARY or ~~INTELLIGENCE SUMMARY.~~

(Erase heading not required.)

of Major W.W.R. Neale A.V.C. D.A.D.V.S. 17 Division

Army Form C. 2118.

Dec '18

Place	Date	Hour	Summary of Events and Information	Remarks and references to Appendices
INCHY	Decr 1-8		Inspection duty. On the 2nd all the mares in the Division were paraded in order that suitable mares for breeding in England might be selected. Only one mare in the Division was considered suitable.	
			On the 4th H.M. The King inspected the Division	
ST GRATIEN	9-12		Left INCHY on the 9th and arrived ST GRATIEN same day. This was a stage for Divisional H.Qrs whilst the Division marched down. Left ST GRATIEN on the 12th and arrived HALLENCOURT the same day.	
HALLENCOURT	13-25		Inspection duty. During this period most of the animals of the Division were standing out in the open and as it was very wet the standings got very bad and the animals fell off in condition. No surplus forage either could be obtained. The animals not nearly so well off as in the forward area.	
— " —	29-31		Classifying animals for Demobilization.	

W.W.R. Neale Major
D.A.D.V.S. 17th Division

D. D. & L., London, E.C.
(A10266) Wt W5300/P713 750,000 2/18 Sch. 52 Forms/C2118/16

January 1919 14/3 19

Army Form C. 2118.

Instructions regarding War Diaries and Intelligence Summaries are contained in F. S. Regs., Part II. and the Staff Manual respectively. Title pages will be prepared in manuscript.

WAR DIARY of Major W.W.R. Neale AVC DADVS. 17 Division
or
~~INTELLIGENCE SUMMARY.~~

(*Erase heading not required.*)

Place	Date	Hour	Summary of Events and Information	Remarks and references to Appendices
HALLENCOURT	Jan? 1–15		Classifying all animals of all units of the Division for Demobilization	
	19		Handed over duties of DADVS. 17th Division to Captain J.T.G. KEPPEL RAVC. and proceeded to VIGNACOURT and took over duties of ADVS V Corps from Lt. Col. G. CONDER D.S.O RAVC. who is being invalided.	

D. D. & L., London, E.C.
(A10266) Wt W5300/P713 750,000 2/18 Sch. 52 Forms/C2118/16

9/3

Instructions regarding War Diaries and Intelligence Summaries are contained in F. S. Regs., Part II. and the Staff Manual respectively. Title pages will be prepared in manuscript.

WAR DIARY or ~~INTELLIGENCE SUMMARY.~~

(Erase heading not required.)

D.A.D.V.S
17 Division
January 20 – 31.

Army Form C. 2118.

Place	Date	Hour	Summary of Events and Information	Remarks and references to Appendices
HALLENCOURT.	20 – 31		assumed duties of acting D.A.D.V.S when Major W.W.R NEALE RAVC proceeded to Fifth Corps H.Q on 19-1-19. (and still conducted duties of O.C. 29 Mobile Veterinary Section)	
	20.		Inspected the "C" class horses of the 78 and 79 BRIGADES of ARTILLERY with the Remount Officer of 17 DIVISION but owing to the Veterinary instruction and classification it was not found possible to include the "C" class horses in the other groups of the Remount department.	
	21.		Inspected with Remount Officer "C" class horses of 52 INFANTRY BRIGADE and converted a C Z animal into an A.Y no other animals from this Brigade being good enough to make "Y" horses.	
	22		attended to Office duty.	
	23.		Inspected at BOURDON. HORSE DEMOBILIZATION CAMP the "Y" animals for Rehabilitation.	

D. D. & L., London, E.C. (10340) Wt W5300/P713 750,000 3/18 E 2688 Forms C/2118/15.

Instructions regarding War Diaries and Intelligence Summaries are contained in F. S. Regs., Part II. and the Staff Manual respectively. Title pages will be prepared in manuscript.

WAR DIARY
or
INTELLIGENCE SUMMARY.
(*Erase heading not required.*)

DADVS
17 Division
January 30-31.

Army Form C. 2118.

Place	Date	Hour	Summary of Events and Information	Remarks and references to Appendices
HALLENCOURT	24		Inspected "C" class horses of 51 INFANTRY BRIGADE but got none good enough to be made "Y" animals. Malleined YORKS + LANCS Horses.	
	~~25~~ 25.		Inspected MACHINE GUN BATTALION animals of the "C" class but got none suitable. 15 D minus mules classified as suit for vice & reclassified to 2 + and 13 C as the animals were only timid and nervous. Malleined the "Y" animals of Divisional H.Q.	
	26.		Malleined 51 FIELD AMBULANCE. Inspected with the Remount Officer 50 INFANTRY BRIGADE "C" animals - negative result.	
	27		Inspected at HANGEST a party of "Y" class horses before entering V. Corps Horse Camp. Rejected two animals for Cataract.	
	28		Office Routine	
	29		do do	

D. D. & L., London, E.C.
(10340) Wt W5300/P713 750,000 3/18 E 2688 Forms/C/2118/15.

Army Form C. 2118.

Instructions regarding War Diaries and Intelligence Summaries are contained in F. S. Regs., Part II. and the Staff Manual respectively. Title pages will be prepared in manuscript.

WAR DIARY
or
INTELLIGENCE SUMMARY.
(Erase heading not required.)

DADVS

17 Division January 30-31

Place	Date	Hour	Summary of Events and Information	Remarks and references to Appendices
HALLENCOURT	30		Selected horses suitable for evacuation to Veterinary Hospital as ~~[illegible]~~ opposed to those animals suitable for the Butcher and Sale to farmers.	
	31.		Inspected HQ horses for reclassification but [illegible] result.	

D. D. & L., London, E.C.
(10340) Wt W5300/P713 750,000 3/18 E 2688 Forms/C/2118/16.

714 DADVS [illegible] Division

WAR DIARY
or
INTELLIGENCE SUMMARY.

(Erase heading not required.)

Army Form C. 2118.

Instructions regarding War Diaries and Intelligence Summaries are contained in F. S. Regs., Part II. and the Staff Manual respectively. Title pages will be prepared in manuscript.

Place	Date	Hour	Summary of Events and Information	Remarks and references to Appendices
COCQUERIL	1–9 Feb.		Lived at COCQUERIL with 27 Mobile Vety Section and visited HALLENCOURT daily to attend to office of DADVS. Attended to Routine work of Mobile Vety Section and DADVS Office. Daily inspections had to be made of animals proceeding to the Corps [illegible] Concentration Camp at BOURDON. Animals [illegible] were of the Y Class for England.	
HALLENCOURT	9–28		Took up residence at Divisional HQ as a Veterinary Officer was sent to assist me. The work was mainly Routine and a great deal of inspecting of Animals before they left the division had to be made especially [illegible] as for the Y Class animals for England. On February 27th a very successful [illegible] of Y Class animals was held at Airaines	

D. D. & L., London, E.C. (10340) Wt W5300/P713 750,000 3/18 E 2688 Forms/C2118/16.

WAR DIARY
or
INTELLIGENCE SUMMARY.
(Erase heading not required.)

Army Form C. 2118.

Instructions regarding War Diaries and Intelligence Summaries are contained in F. S. Regs., Part II. and the Staff Manual respectively. Title pages will be prepared in manuscript.

V DADVS

Place	Date	Hour	Summary of Events and Information	Remarks and references to Appendices
HALLENCOURT	9.28		and very good prices were realised. On February 12th I was officially appointed DADVS. Apart from inspections of animals necessary to demobilisation there was nothing of note to relate. [illegible] DADVS 17 Div	

D. D. & L., London, E.C.
(10340) Wt W5300/P713 750,000 3/18 E 2688 Forms/C2118/16.

Army Form C. 2118.

Instructions regarding War Diaries and Intelligence Summaries are contained in F. S. Regs., Part II. and the Staff Manual respectively. Title pages will be prepared in manuscript.

WAR DIARY
or
INTELLIGENCE SUMMARY.

(*Erase heading not required.*)

9 March [illegible]

Place	Date	Hour	Summary of Events and Information	Remarks and references to Appendices
HALLENCOURT	1-31		Work was purely routine – Inspecting and re-classifying animals either for England or for sale on the Continent. The animals were being rapidly demobilized and there was every reason to ensure [illegible] [illegible] of the men.	
			X [illegible] animals for Army of Occupation were [illegible] and towards the end of the month only a small number of animals were left and they were necessary for use in [illegible] [illegible] the Cadre Park	
			As the animals left reduction in the RAVC became to take place and by 31-3-19 all the RAVC had either been demobilized or posted to units in the case of retainable men. The Mobile Vety Section was reduced to cadre strength and [illegible] [illegible] Commander [illegible] the seven other Ranks forming the Cadre joined [illegible] [illegible] HQ.	
			[illegible signature]	

D. D. & L., London, E.C. (10340) Wt W5300/P713 750,000 3/18 E 2688 Forms/C2118/16.

www.ingramcontent.com/pod-product-compliance
Lightning Source LLC
Chambersburg PA
CBHW081428160426
43193CB00013B/2217
9781474510240